A Professional's Guide
to
RAILWAY
PHOTOGRAPHY

A Professional's Guide to RAILWAY PHOTOGRAPHY

Roger Siviter ARPS

Silver Link Publishing Ltd

**To my wife Christina without whose help
none of this would have been possible**

First published as *A Handbook of Railway Photography* by
David & Charles in 1983, and as *A Photographer's Guide to
Railways* by Peerage Books in 1989
This revised edition first published 2002

British Library Cataloguing in Publication Data

A catalogue record for this book is available from the
British Library.

ISBN 1 85794 195 0

Silver Link Publishing Ltd
The Trundle
Ringstead Road
Great Addington
Kettering
Northants NN14 4BW

Tel/Fax: 01536 330588
email: sales@nostalgiacollection.com
Website: www.nostalgiacollection.com

Except where otherwise credited, all photographs are by the
author.

Printed and bound in Great Britain

Frontispiece On 20 April 1983 'Peak' Class diesel-electric
locomotive No 45109 approaches Kettering station with a
morning St Pancras to Nottingham train. This picture illustrates
that on a dull day it is necessary to have strong foreground shapes
to highlight the train. The platform canopy, lamps and rails all
lead to the main subject, which is also framed by the signal box
and signals.

*Camera: Nikon FM with 50mm lens. Exposure: 1/250th sec at
f4.5. Film: Ilford XP1 rated at 400 ASA and developed in XP1
chemicals.*

Contents

Introduction   **7**

1 Choice of equipment   **9**
  Camera formats and types   9
  Films   11
  Supplementary or interchangeable lenses 12
  Motor drives and power winders   17
  Filters   18
  Lens hoods   20
  Tripods   20
  Exposure meters   20

2 Monochrome darkroom work   **23**
  The darkroom   23
  Developing a negative   23
  Printing and enlarging   24
  Glazing   30
  Spotting   30
  Shading and dodging   32
  Double printing   33
  Composing on the enlarger baseboard   33
  Print quality   34
  Mounting and presentation   36

3 Colour photography   **38**

4 Railway photography –
general principles   **41**
  Steam   41
  Diesel   43

  Electric   45
  Miniature railways   45

5 Style, composition and
techniques   **50**
  Style   50
  Composition   51
  Techniques   68

6 Weather and lighting   **99**
  Weather   99
  Lighting   105

7 Night photography   **110**
  Flashlight   110
  Available light   113

8 Common faults and remedies   **116**

9 General information   **122**
  Keeping records   122
  Storing films and prints   122
  Care of equipment   123
  Submitting material for publication   123
  Learning more   124
  Photographing abroad   125
  Do's and don'ts   126

Glossary   **127**
Index   **128**

The railway scene at night can be very photogenic as witnessed from this study of a pair of English Electric Class 40s, Nos 40160 and 40063, at Crewe station on 28 December 1982. The cab lights and strong station lights all help to add sparkle to this nocturnal scene.

Camera: Nikon FM with 50mm lens. Exposure: 40 seconds at f5.6. Film: Ilford XP1 rated at 400 ASA, developed in XP1 chemicals.

Introduction

When I first became interested in railways I used to buy *The Railway Magazine, Trains Illustrated*, etc, and apart from the very interesting and informative articles, what really impressed me were the many fine photographs contained inside their covers.

Inspired by these pictures and armed with my first camera – a Purma Special (which has now become something of a collector's item, having been the first all-plastic camera) – I set out to try my hand at photographing trains, determined to emulate the photographic names of the day.

The early results were not good, and as time went on I soon began to realise that railway photography must surely be one of the most challenging aspects of photography, yet one that can be very enjoyable and at times rewarding.

The essence of railway photography is being able to preserve for ever on film a magic moment that would otherwise, with the passage of time, be a vague memory. The photographic print and slide preserve the past, not only for the photographer but for the countless number of people who enjoy looking at railway pictures. But it is much more than that, for the photograph is also important from the historical point of view. The invention of photography must rank as one of the most important scientific developments of the 19th century. We can now *see* the history of the last hundred years or so, a thing that was almost impossible before photography except through sketches and paintings. Until the first photographs were created in the 1850s only the artist was able to record the past, and this was not always very accurate. This of course applied equally well to railways.

Although many railway photographs were taken before the end of the 19th century by some notable pioneers, it was not until the early 1900s that the art of railway photography really began to develop through the work of such photographers as T. F. Budden, Rev T. B. Parley, F. E. Mackay and H. Gordon Tidey, and later by Maurice Earley, who did so much for this art form and whose splendid GWR pictures were an inspiration to so many of us. Mr Earley was also responsible for the running of the Railway Photographic Society, a postal portfolio club that helped to produce so many excellent photographers.

The earliest photographers used plate cameras, which were extremely heavy and cumbersome to carry around, especially on lineside trips, but which produced prints of fine quality. By the late 1920s and early 1930s roll-film cameras began to take over, making lineside work much easier and more practical. (The famous Rollieflex twin-lens reflex camera first appeared in 1928.)

Another very important development around that time was the introduction of the 35mm camera by Leica, a camera that could be carried in one's pocket. It was a far cry from the plate cameras used by railway photographers a few years earlier. Meanwhile films were improving to keep pace with the smaller cameras, and very good results were possible even with the new 35mm cameras

Thus in the space of a few years the improvement in cameras, especially in size and weight, and the use of roll film instead of glass plates allowed the railway photographer to get to locations and take photographs that would have been virtually impossible for his predecessors.

By the 1930s railway photography began to be much more pictorial. Until then, fine lineside action photographs, in which the train was all-important to the exclusion of almost everything else, were traditional, but photographers, led notably by Eric Treacy, began to incorporate the whole railway scene into the photograph, with station shots, shed shots, landscape shots, night shots, etc. The 1930s must have been one of the most exciting times on the railways with crack expresses on the four main lines, and the development of large and magnificent steam engines and beautiful rolling-stock. The 'Coronation Scot' must surely have been a wonderful sight as it stormed up Shap; it is a great pity that some of today's high-quality colour films were not available then. However, thanks to the efforts of the photographers of the 1930s we do have very many fine monochrome photographs of those halcyon days.

This trend in pictorialism continued until the demise of steam on British Railways, when a wave of new photographers led by Colin Gifford started what was to become known as the New Approach. This made artistic use of natural lighting, particularly *contre-jour*, people, reflections, framing the subject and a whole host of fresh ideas that created a new, exciting and very atmospheric type of railway photograph. This style is very useful when photographing modern traction. Because of the lack of exhaust and the other dynamic aspects of steam traction, something needs to be added to create atmosphere, but more of that in a later chapter.

All these varying aspects of photography are discussed in this book, which I hope will encourage people to record today's railway scene on film for tomorrow, since by then it will be history.

I would like to thank the many railway photographers past and present who through their efforts have preserved our railways on film for all of us to enjoy, and all railwaymen, professional and amateur, who make it all possible. In particular, in connection with the preparation of this book, I would like to express my thanks to Bob Dallow FRPS AFIAP for his advice and help, to Malcolm Ranieri FRPS, to Joan Wappett for sterling work at the typewriter, and last but not least Will Adams and the team at Silver Link.

1
Choice of equipment

Camera formats and types

Most photographers must have asked themselves at one time or another 'What format shall I use?' There is never an easy answer to this, as all sizes have advantages and disadvantages. Remember that there is no such thing as the perfect camera, but what you can do is to find the equipment that is the most suited to your own personal requirements and stick to it. Having settled on the system that suits you and that produces the results you require, it could be a mistake to change. You will find that most of the top professional and amateur photographers have been using the same equipment for years, with consistently good results, which must be a good example for all of us to follow.

With regard to size, I mainly use 35mm single lens reflex cameras and equipment because this suits my requirements, but I do on occasions use larger format cameras, as will be seen from some of the photographs in this book. The important point about railway photography is that it is mainly *action* photography, which means that whatever size of equipment we chose to use, be it large or small format, our cameras must have a shutter speed as fast as 1/250th second at the very least.

Let us now consider the main advantages and disadvantages of the different camera formats.

35mm

A very large selection of cameras and lenses is available in this format over a wide price range. This size is excellent for taking colour slides and many 35mm projectors and ancillary equipment are available on the photographic market.

Many problems can arise when doing black and white work. In this size it needs a far greater degree of enlargement compared to larger formats and great care must be taken in the development of films. Figure 1 compares the different negative sizes from 35mm to 6 x 7cm, and it will be seen from this the far greater enlargement needed by 35mm compared to, say, 6 x 6cm (2¼in square) to make a reasonable enlargement.

Medium and large formats, 645, 6 x 6cm, 6 x 7cm

All cameras in these formats use 120 size film, and these formats are extremely good for black and white work, enabling you to use faster films and achieve very fine results.

The 645 system is often called the ideal format, with a side/length ratio (6 x 4.5cm) that comes very close to matching standard paper sizes, especially in the popular 20.3 x 25.4cm (8 x 10in) paper size. This means less trimming with enlargements, which means that the full negative area can be used efficiently and economically.

There is not such a wide selection of cameras, lenses and projectors, etc, on the market compared with the 35mm size, and most of the equipment, using 120 size roll film, is in the higher price range.

The conclusion that maybe one could draw from this is that the larger formats are best used for monochrome work and 35mm for colour slides, as many photographers already do. However, this in turn can create problems, not the least of which is financial. Thus it comes down to individual tastes and requirements.

One idea, which is proving popular among railway photographers, is to mount two cameras together on a single frame with their shutters linked for simultaneous monochrome and colour exposures. If you try out this

Figure 1: Comparative dimensions of negatives in actual sizes.

Figure 2: A method of mounting two cameras for taking simultaneous monochrome and colour photographs. The diagram shows two cameras (of different formats) mounted together on a single frame supported by a tripod. A cable release is mounted to each shutter and the two releases are clamped together to enable the shutters to be fired simultaneously.

system, remember to make sure that the lenses on both cameras are of the equivalent focal lengths. Do not mix the lenses around, for example by using a telephoto on one camera and a wide angle on the other, as this will cause obvious problems.

With regard to cameras larger than the 6 x 7cm size, although superb results are obtainable with these very large format sizes, some of which often referred to as press cameras and usually date from past years, the disadvantages outweigh the advantages for the railway photographer of today. Indeed, it would only be in huge enlargements that you would be able to see the difference between them and the smaller format, such is the improvement in material and equipment in the smaller sizes in the last few decades.

I have also not referred to the 127 or smaller sizes of camera often taking cassette film because arguably, with one or two exceptions, while fine for family albums they are limited in this type of photography, with limited shutter speeds and producing very small colour negatives and prints.

Once you have decided on the format you are going to use, it is time to consider the camera types that are available in the various sizes.

Single lens reflex (SLR)

This system is particularly suited to action photography, and thus to railway photography. Principally this is because the image seen in the camera's viewfinder is the image that passes through the taking lens and is recorded on the film, and it appears the right way up in eye-level viewfinders, as on 35mm cameras. However, in both the larger format SLR and the twin lens reflex camera (see below) the camera is held at waist level and viewed from above. In this type of viewfinder, the image appears as the reverse of the actual scene (although it is recorded the correct way round on the film). On most makes of this type of camera, to rectify this and give the user the convenience of eye level viewfinding (as on 35mm cameras) the waist-level viewfinder can be exchanged for an eye-level prism.

The other big advantage of the SLR system is that all the lenses are interchangeable, which gives tremendous scope in the composition of pictures.

Twin lens reflex (TLR)

The principal of this system is that one lens is used for taking the picture and the other for viewing and focusing (both lenses having the same focal length and being coupled together). These cameras are available only in the 6 x 6cm size (2¼in) and are now only manufactured by a few firms, the most famous being Yashica and Mamiya. A feature of the Mamiya system is that the lenses are interchangeable. The most famous of all twin lens cameras, the Rollieflex, has only ceased production in recent years and many of these fine cameras are still available on the second-hand market.

Viewfinder cameras

These cameras, at one time available in all the different formats, are now, with one or two exceptions, confined to the 35mm size. Most cameras have fixed lenses, these being popularly known as compacts, because of their compact size, but on some 35mm cameras, namely the famous Leica M series and the Russian Fed and Zorki, the lenses are interchangeable.

Viewing is not through the lens as in the SLR system, but simply through a viewfinder, usually set above the lens. This means that you do not get on the film exactly what you see in the viewfinder, which can be a disadvantage in action photography and in close-up detail work.
Focusing is either by a range-finder coupled to the lens and viewfinder, or on the less sophisticated models by simply working out the subject distance and setting it on the distance scale on the lens barrel.

One of the main advantages of this type of camera is that, unlike the SLR with a return mirror (for viewing), there is less likelihood of any shake being caused after the release of the shutter. However, with today's SLR cameras this problem has largely been overcome by improved design of the mirror mechanism.

Digital cameras

New technology means that with a digital rather than film image you are far more in control than with traditional cameras. The camera's LCD screen allows you to view the picture as soon as you've taken it, and with a static subject you can retake it as many times as you like until you are satisfied with the result. That apart, the technique for taking the photographs is the same as with a conventional camera.

Once taken, the image is stored on the camera's 'memory card', and once full this can simply be removed and replaced with another. You can subsequently manipulate the images on your computer, using a variety of software packages that offer easy techniques for enhancing pictures – improving the colours, sharpening the image, and of course removing unwanted intrusions like the proverbial telegraph pole in the chimney! You can then print off as many copies as you require, using a high-quality colour printer and photographic-quality paper. Once in the computer, the digital image can also easily be used in e-mails or to produce birthday cards, calendars, etc. Once the images have been downloaded, the memory card can by wiped for re-use. If you do not have a computer, dedicated photo printers are available that print directly from the camera's memory card.

The majority of digital cameras are 'compact' models, although SLRs are becoming available; for serious photographers the latter are best, offering interchangeable lenses and producing very high-quality results, but they are very much more expensive. Indeed, all digital cameras are more expensive than their 35mm equivalents (although of course there are no film or processing charges), their price depending on the number of 'pixels', the minute coloured squares that form the basic element of a digital image. These can range from 300,000 pixels for a cheaper camera to many millions ('megapixels') for a more expensive one. The more pixels, the greater the image quality, and resolutions are indicated by the number of pixels across and down the image, eg 640 x 480. Most cameras have the facility to vary the resolution between shots, allowing variable use of the available memory. A basic megapixel camera will produce good-quality images up to 6 x 4in.

Better cameras include a useful 'docking' device, allowing the camera to be connected to the computer so that images can be downloaded and the camera batteries recharged at the same time. Others offer zoom lenses and built-in flashes.

Experts recommend that, if you purchase a digital camera, you buy an extra memory card with greater capacity that the one supplied. Rechargeable battery packs are also a must, and cheaper than using large quantities of disposable batteries.

On the subject of digital technology, if you do not fancy a digital camera, a scanner connected to your computer could be used to produce a digital image of a conventionally taken photograph, allowing the use of the manipulation techniques described above.

Films

There are so many different types of film available on the market today that space does not permit a detailed description of every one; the list below provides a few examples (from slow to fast speed ratings) of both monochrome and colour emulsions.

Films are rated as follows:

Slow – under 100 ASA
Medium – under 400 ASA
Fast – 400 ASA and over

Slow films are very fine grained and sharp, giving high contrast. Medium speed films are the all-rounders, combining good sharpness and fine grain with a fast enough speed for the majority of conditions. Fast films have lower contrast than slow and medium speed films, and by using certain developers the speed of the film can be increased. This means that the film can be under-exposed (within limits) in poor lighting conditions but can produce good negatives by special developers, a decided advantage in bad weather.

35mm black and white films

Ilford Pan F, 50 ASA: A fine-grain film that can produce excellent results. In addition, because of its 50 ASA speed rating, it is quite useful for action photography.

Ilford FP4 and Kodak Plus-X, 125 ASA: Both these medium speed films give very good resolution and excellent tonal quality and are ideally suited for railway photography, especially action photography.

Kodak Tri-X, 400 ASA: This is a fast film giving good grain and sharpness, but needs careful exposure and development to achieve the best results.

Ilford XP2, 400 ASA: This high-speed film gives results comparable to slower general-purpose films and can be uprated if necessary, but it is important to develop to the manufacturer's instructions.

35mm colour reversal film for transparencies

(Processing is included in price of these films except where otherwise stated.)

Kodachrome 25 KM135, 25 ASA: In the photographic world this film is regarded as the finest available; however, railway photographers may find it a little too slow for most of their work.

Fuji Velvia, 50 ASA: This very fine grained film gives good colour contrast and resolution.

Kodachrome 64 KR135, 64 ASA: Another excellent film giving good contrast and resolution, and fast enough for the majority of railway photography.

Fuji Sensia, 100 ASA: Faster than the Fuji Velvia, it still gives fine grain and resolution.

Kodachrome 200, 200 ASA: This film also gives good contrast and resolution; although not as fine grained as the Kodachrome 64, it is ideal for traction photography.

35mm colour negative film

Kodak Gold, 100 ASA: This excellent colour negative film gives good resolution and contrast and, because it is a reasonably fast film, is ideal for all types of railway photography.

120 (roll film) – black and white film for larger formats

Ilford FP4, 125 ASA: This is arguably the finest medium speed film on the market, giving excellent contrast and resolution coupled with beautiful tonal quality.

Kodak Tri-X, 400 ASA: A high-speed film ideal for use with the larger format. Excellent for action photography, having minimal grain and good sharpness.

Ilford HP5, 400 ASA: Another excellent high-speed film that can be uprated with good results.

120 (roll film) – colour reversal film for larger formats

Fuji Velvia, 50 ASA: A very fine grained film.

Fuji Provia, 100 ASA: A faster film, but still having a very fine grain.

120 (roll film) – colour negative film for larger formats

Kodak Gold, 100 ASA: A good all-round film with a fast enough speed for most occasions.

Films for night photography

Fujichrome 64T: Available for both 35mm and 120 formats, this film is tungsten balanced to avoid excessive greens and yellows.

Number of exposures

Summarised below are the numbers of exposures that can be taken with the various camera sizes and film lengths. This is relevant to the choice of equipment discussed above.

35mm: Both black and white negative and colour slide films usually come in 20 and 36 exposure sizes, but colour negative film (for prints) can be obtained in 12, 24 and 36 exposure sizes.

645: Black and white, 15 and 30 exposures; colour, 15 exposures.

6 x 6cm: Black and white, 12 and 24 exposures; colour 12 exposures.

6 x 7cm: Black and white, 10 and 20 exposures; colour 10 exposures.

The above are commercial film sizes that can be bought at any photographic store. (Some older cameras giving other formats and exposures on 120 size film occasionally come on to the second-hand market.)

Motor drives can be used with all the above formats, and on some of the cameras special interchangeable backs can be fitted enabling the camera to shoot up to 250 exposures without having to change films. For this purpose certain film can be bought in bulk length, generally only through the more specialist photographic dealers, which is then loaded into the interchangeable backs. A point worth noting is that as 35mm film comes loaded in cassettes, once these cassettes are empty they can be loaded from bulk film, although this can prove tricky and must be done in a darkroom. The alternative is to use a special bulk film loader, which usually comes complete with reloadable cassettes. Nonetheless many people still find it more convenient to buy ready-loaded cassettes.

Supplementary or interchangeable lenses

Cameras are generally fitted with what is called a standard or normal lens, indicating one of between 40mm and 58mm focal length on a 35mm camera, 75mm to 80mm on the 645 and 6 x 6cm sizes, and 90mm to 105mm on the 6 x 7cm format. The focal length of a standard lens produces the most natural perspective image in relation to the picture

Above In this scene on the Waterside colliery system on 30 August 1973, Barclay 0-4-0 saddle tank No 19 hauls a load of coal from Pennyvenie colliery to the washery at Dunaskin. Notice the cloud and smoke effect – one of the main features of the picture – which has been heavily emphasised by the use of a yellow filter.

Camera: Nikkormat 35mm SLR plus 35mm lens and yellow filter. Exposure: 1/500th sec at f5.6. Film: Ilford FP4 rated at 200 ASA, developed in Acuspecial.

Right Figure 3: A line drawing of the photograph on which is shown the comparative areas covered by various lens sizes from medium wide angle (whole of the picture) through to long telephoto. The sizes are in 35mm format, but in this section comparative lens sizes are described for medium and large formats.

It will be noted that the angles of perspective in the receding parallels are markedly different from wide angle to telephoto pictures, and that the cropping of photographs does not give the same effect. In telephoto shots the rear three-quarter view of the train is not much lower than the front, giving a bunched-up appearance, while in standard or wide angle shots the end of the train diminishes in size more naturally.

area, its angle of vision being the equivalent of the view seen by the average human eye.

If you have chosen a camera system that enables you to use supplementary or interchangeable lenses (ie either a single lens reflex, or certain makes of twin lens reflex and viewfinder cameras), by using lenses of different focal lengths you will be able to vary the angle of vision. In other words, if you use a wide angle lens the view is widened and the subject matter is proportionately smaller. If you use a telephoto or long lens the view is narrowed and the subject matter is enlarged. By using a variety of different lens sizes, as many railway photographers do, you can bring exciting new possibilities to your photography.

Before discussing in detail the various advantages and disadvantages of wide angle, telephoto and zoom lenses, there are two photographic terms that you must understand, since they are extremely relevant to this section. The first is **aperture**, which is the circular opening within the camera lens that controls the amount of light reaching the film. Most apertures are variable, the size of the lens opening being indicated by the 'f' number. The other term is **depth of field**, which is the distance between the nearest and furthest points of the subject that are acceptably sharp. Depth of field can be increased by using small apertures (large f numbers), short focal length lenses (wide angle), or by simply taking the photograph from further away. The depth of field is reduced by the use of large apertures (small f numbers), telephoto lenses and by photographing subjects as close as is possible.

Wide angle lenses

When using the more extreme wide angle lenses a certain amount of distortion of the subject is inevitable. This is especially noticeable when taking pictures of, for example, static locomotives on shed. This is because the wider the angle of vision, the flatter the field, which means that the subject nearest to the lens, usually the front end of the locomotive, appears a great deal larger than the subject at the rear of the picture. This can be avoided by using the wide angle lens that is closest to the standard lens on whatever format is being used. With this size of lens, it is doubtful if any distortion would be discernible on the picture, even to the experienced and trained eye. Indeed, some people use this size of lens as their standard lens.

The advantages of using a medium wide angle lens are numerous. They are excellent for use in confined spaces such as stations and locomotive sheds and are useful when there is more than one locomotive pulling a train and you want to get a good picture of a double or, as is sometimes the case on enthusiasts' trains, a triple header. Because of

the great depth of field given by wide-angle lenses, they are very suitable for photographing trains on the move when accurate focusing may be difficult. One very important point to remember is that it is more difficult to compute and manufacture wide angle lenses than telephoto types; if you want good results with a wide angle, spend as much as you can afford when buying one. The old saying 'you only gets what you pay for' certainly applies to the purchase of these lenses.

Recommended wide angle lens sizes are as follows:

Camera format	35mm	645 and 6 x 6cm	6 x 7cm
Lens size	35mm	50/55mm	75mm

Telephoto lenses

Telephoto or long lenses are the opposite of wide-angle lenses in that they reduce the depth of field and foreshorten the subject matter, although this is not very noticeable on moderate focal length lenses. In the 35mm format an 85mm lens is perhaps more useful than any other telephoto lens, as it brings the subject just that bit closer without the 'bunching' effect created by longer telephoto lenses. Couple this with the fast maximum aperture found on this size of lens and you have an excellent combination for action photography.

The most popular of all telephoto lenses is the 135mm in the 35mm format (see the table below for the equivalent lens sizes in the different formats.) These lenses usually have a fairly fast maximum aperture of around f2.8 or even faster. This is very useful for action photography (where high shutter speeds are required) and also on dull days when the light is poor. This size of lens is also very good for taking pictures when a train is in an awkward location, for example on a bridge or viaduct surrounded by a deep valley (as is so often the case), and you are unable to get

Patrick Stirling's 8-foot single 4-2-2 No 1 of 1870 makes a fine sight as it storms out of Loughborough on the Great Central Railway with a train for Rothley on 13 June 1982. This beautiful engine was on temporary loan from the National Railway Museum at York. By enclosing the train in a cutting, flanked by tall trees, and by taking the engine nearly head-on with a 135mm lens, I succeeded in conveying the effect of compressed power. This is helped by a low viewpoint and a vertical format, which shows the towering exhaust to greater advantage. As I took this picture on the shadow side, I allowed half a stop over-exposure. This, coupled with the reflected light off the ballast, gave some detail in the shadows, which was brought out in the printing stage.

Camera: Nikon FM with 135mm lens plus yellow filter.
Exposure: 1/500th sec at f6.3. Film: Ilford FP4 rated at 200 ASA, developed in Acuspecial.

No 60009 *Union of South Africa* storms up to Plean Junction south of Stirling with an Edinburgh-Aberdeen special on 18 April 1981. Sunlight from behind throws up the exhaust with dramatic edge-lighting against a pale sky, and renders the two subjects almost as silhouettes. The effect of compressed power is increased by the use of a short telephoto lens to 'bunch up' slightly the perspective of the coaches. Notice how the slope of the semaphore leads the eye to the chimney of the locomotive, which although it is near the centre of the composition is visually drawn to the right by the signals.

Camera: Nikon FM with 85mm lens plus yellow filter. Exposure: 1/500th sec at f6.3. Film: Ilford FP4 rated at 160 ASA, developed in Aculux.

near enough to take a picture with a standard lens; by using a 135mm telephoto lens you will bring the scene almost three times nearer to you, enabling you to take a picture that you would otherwise have missed.

The longer telephoto lenses give a terrific effect of compressed power when you take a picture of a train front end on, especially when taking pictures of steam engines. Because of the foreshortening of the subject by the lens, the plume of smoke from the locomotive chimney very often appears to rise to the heavens, giving the appearance of a volcano on the move. There are two very important points to bear in mind when using telephoto lenses. First always use as high a shutter speed as possible, certainly never less than a 1/250th sec. This is because all telephoto lenses are physically longer than standard or wide angle lenses and are therefore harder to hold steady and more prone to camera shake. Certainly with the very long lenses, it is worthwhile using a pistol grip shutter release, or even a tripod and cable release. No doubt in the course of time you will meet people who say they can hand-hold long lenses at shutter speeds of 1/60th sec, 1/30th sec or even slower. Before believing them, you might ask to see their pictures!

The second important point is that because of the shallow depth of field of long lenses, focusing must always be extremely accurate, allowing for the fact that however far away the front of an approaching train may be, the back will be 500 feet or so further away if it is almost head on.

Recommended telephoto lens sizes are as follows:

Camera format	35mm	645 and 6 x 6cm	6 x 7cm
Short	85mm	100 to 135mm	150mm
Medium	135mm	150 to 180mm	200mm
Long	200mm	250 to 300mm	300mm

Zoom lenses

It is only in recent years that zoom lenses have been manufactured for use with still cameras, having been originally made for use on cine cameras. In theory the idea of a zoom lens for a still camera is ideal – to be able to move from one focal length to another without having to change lenses is obviously very useful for railway action photography – but in practice there are certain drawbacks. Many zoom lenses have fairly slow maximum apertures, which can cause obvious problems. For example, when photographing a moving train in poor lighting conditions you require a high shutter speed and therefore a fast maximum aperture.

It is also worth bearing in mind that some zoom lenses are bulky and heavy, and again require to be used with high shutter speeds to avoid camera shake. It is very important to note that unless top-quality zoom lenses are used, which are usually expensive (extremely expensive in the large format sizes), the quality is, as a general rule, not up to the standard of fixed focal length lenses. This may not be too noticeable if your work is mainly confined to taking colour slides for projection, but could be a critical factor in monochrome and colour print work where enlarging and cropping are so important. In addition, if you are planning on submitting your slides or monochrome prints to publishers for possible reproduction in magazines and books, high-quality material, in focus and with good definition, is essential.

If you are going to invest in a zoom lens, buy the very best you can afford, make sure it is not too heavy and bulky, and that it has a reasonably fast maximum aperture, so important in railway photography. There are so many zooms of different focal lengths on the market today that it is difficult to recommend any particular size, but try to get a lens that suits your particular needs, and one that is comfortable to hold and has an easy action in use.

Lens converters

Converters extend the focal length of a lens and are intended for use with cameras with detachable lenses, the converter fitting between the camera body and the lens. As a rule, converters come in three different sizes, 1½x, 2x or 3x. If you fit them on to your standard lens, say the 50mm of a 35mm camera, the 1½x converter will give you 50 per cent more focal length – 75mm. The 2x will give you double the focal length – 100mm – and the 3x converter three times the focal length – 150mm.

Converters work in the same way with lenses of any focal length, but the picture quality achieved with them is usually at its best when they are used with lenses of focal lengths between 50mm and 200mm on a 35mm camera, and 75mm to 300mm on the larger formats.

The focusing distance is unaffected by using a lens converter. If the minimum focusing distance is 3 feet without the converter, it is still 3 feet with the converter fitted.

There are certain important disadvantages when using a converter. Not only does it multiply the focal length of the lens, it also multiplies the f number of the lens. If your lens aperture is set at f2, a 2x converter halves the aperture to f4. This means that as less light is coming into the lens, you will need to use a slower shutter speed – half the speed for a 2x – in compensation, which can cause problems, especially in action photography.

Another important disadvantage is that the picture quality achieved with a lens converter is rarely up to the standard of a prime lens. However, having said that, lens converters are not usually as expensive to buy as new lenses and it can be very convenient to have one tucked away in your camera bag to film that viaduct or bridge scene that is just too far away or not convenient for your range of lenses. Like most things in photography, buy the best you can afford from a reputable manufacturer. If your camera is automatic or has a built-in meter, make sure you can use the converter with the camera's metering system.

Motor drives and power winders

When a motor drive or power winder is fitted to your camera, once you have fired the shutter of the camera the film is automatically wound on. This means that your eye need never move from the viewfinder when, for example, you are taking a sequence of action shots, as would be the case if you were winding on the film by hand. You can therefore concentrate completely on the sequence, and you will not miss that vital master shot, as can happen when you take your eye away from the viewfinder even for a split second.

The motor drive has the added facility of continuous firing of the shutter, which means that you can just keep the shutter depressed and it will fire off automatically at, for example, seven frames in 2 seconds. However, you may prefer to use it just as a power winder, and be more selective in choosing when to take your pictures. Naturally, you have to be careful not to waste too much film, especially when using colour, but it is better to waste one or two frames to get the shot that really pleases you. You might find that in a sequence of around four to six shots you will have two or three potentially good ones, especially the three-quarter rear or 'going away' shot, which is often so easy and convenient to take when using a power winder. Power winders are available for most makes of single lens reflex cameras in all the format sizes. In addition, some cameras are now on the market with built-in power winders.

Some photographers would argue against the use a power winder at all, and, indeed, very many fine action pictures are taken without using one. However, they make action photography so much easier, and anything that makes railway photography easier is very welcome.

Filters

Filters are useful accessories in both monochrome and colour photography and are sometimes essential to obtain certain effects.

First let us deal with their use in monochrome work. Black and white film does not respond to colours in the same way as the human eye, and to counteract this we can use various colour filters. An obvious example is when we are taking pictures of trains in landscape settings with blue sky and white clouds. If we photograph the scene without using the appropriate filter fitted to the lens of the camera, we will find that on the finished print that the beautiful blue sky and lovely white clouds are not there and that the sky appears to be a white mass. The more we print or burn in the sky at the printing stage, the more grain we get on our finished print without ever really getting the correct sky so important in a good landscape picture. Thus, in order to get good sky and cloud effect on negatives, filters correct the colour receptiveness of the monochrome film.

This is obviously very important when taking pictures of steam locomotives at work, and to get the very best steam and smoke effects we must use a yellow filter. There is nothing worse than to photograph a steam locomotive hard at work giving off a splendid exhaust, only to find that because of the lack of a filter it has not been fully reproduced on the negative, and no amount of burning-in at the printing stage can rectify it. Remember when using filters that most of them reduce the light that enters the camera lens, so the exposure needs to be lengthened. For example, a yellow filter usually increases the exposure by 2x, which means that you must alter your exposure accordingly by either reducing the shutter speed by half or opening up the lens aperture by one stop (which doubles the amount of light through the lens). Thus, if you are taking a subject at 1/250th sec at f8 and decide to use a yellow filter, you must either open the lens aperture by one stop to f5.6 and keep the shutter speed at 1/250th sec, or decrease the shutter speed to 1/125th sec and keep the aperture at f8. If you do not, you will finish up with a thin, under-exposed negative that may present difficulties at the printing stage. If your camera is fitted with through the lens metering (TTL), as a great many are today, when a filter is fitted to the lens the meter will take into account the reduced light and give the correct exposure reading. However, if your camera is fitted with a meter that does not take a reading through the lens, or it is not fitted with one and you simply use a separate meter, you must remember to take the filter into account in taking a light reading and alter the exposure accordingly. It is worth noting that filters act as very good lens protectors, especially against rain or snow or even accidents.

A yellow filter can be used for black and white work all the time, the only exception being when the light is so poor that you need the extra one stop exposure to get a reasonable picture.

Here are details of filters that the railway photographer will find useful for black and white work:

Ultraviolet filter: Also used for colour photography, this absorbs ultraviolet rays and cuts down on haze and fog, while generally not altering the exposure.

Climbing Hatton bank near Warwick on 13 September 1981 is a Class 47 diesel-electric with a northbound passenger train. The whole point of this picture is the remarkable cloud effect, which has been dramatised by the use of a yellow filter. If no filter had been used the sky would have been almost white, and in consequence the whole scene would have looked very flat. Instead, the sky detail, together with the church, gives an almost Constable-like effect. These sorts of detail are very important in any picture, but even more so when photographing modern traction because of the obvious lack of exhaust. Note also the overall rhythm of rounded shapes and the way the bushes echo the shape of the clouds.

This picture also illustrates the usefulness of a short telephoto lens when filming action/landscape pictures. On a lens of this size there is little, if any, distortion or 'bunching up' compared with a longer telephoto lens, and by using a lens slightly longer than standard I was able to be far enough back to get a more balanced composition. Had I been any nearer, the balance and composition of the picture would have been considerably altered.

When using lenses of this size you still get a reasonable depth of field when working with fairly wide apertures, and in this case, at f8, a good depth of field.

Camera: Nikon FM with 85mm lens plus yellow filter.
Exposure: 1/500th sec at f8. Film: Ilford XP1 rated at 400 ASA, developed in XP1 chemicals.

Yellow filter: This filter absorbs the blue wavelengths, making areas of blue sky appear darker. It is ideal in bringing out good contrast between blue skies and clouds and the foreground, and for bringing out steam locomotive smoke effects. It usually increases the exposure by 2x.

Red filter: This has a similar effect to a yellow filter, only more so, and is ideal for dramatic cloud effects. The only problem is that it usually increases exposure by 4x, and in consequence needs a fast film.

Filters are necessary in colour work because colour film, unlike the human eye, does not have the ability to adapt to different light sources. If a colour photograph is being taken on a cloudy but bright day with some blue sky around, the colour balance will tend towards the blue and our subject will have an overall bluish tinge. This also applies when photographing a subject under side or back lighting conditions, for the shadows tend to come out a bluish colour; this is because the shaded areas receive most of their light from the blue sky. To correct this and get the colour balance right we need to use the appropriate filter.

There are two especially important filters that the railway photographer will need to employ for general use. One is the skylight filter, which considerably reduces the excessive bluishness that frequently occurs in outdoor colour photography and is ideal for general work. The other is the ultraviolet filter (which can also be used for monochrome work); this cuts out haze and generally makes the picture more distinct, and is essential when photographing near water or in haze.

Exposure is generally not affected by the use of either of these two filters. Too many good slides have been marred because of incorrect colour balance, something that can be avoided by using the appropriate filter.

Many special filters are also available, most of which would not be much use in railway photography, but one that could be of use is the polarising filter. This makes colours appear brighter, clearer and with better contrast, and is particularly effective when photographing landscapes with blue skies; the sky will appear extremely blue, which could change an ordinary picture into a 'master' shot. However, one problem for railway photographers when using a polarising filter is that the exposure is increased, which may cause problems when photographing trains in action with the slower emulsion colour films.

Last but not least, always remember to change to the appropriate filter for whatever film you are using, especially if you have been photographing in black and white and change to colour. It is not unknown for people to shoot off a roll of colour film with a yellow filter still on the lens!

Lens hoods

Lens hoods are very often overlooked by photographers, yet are such a simple and important accessory. They are either screwed or clipped to the front of the lens and their main purpose is to shield the lens against direct sunlight, thus preventing excessive lens flare when the film is exposed, something that has spoiled many a photograph. Naturally, they are very useful when taking pictures against the light, and also act as a protector against rain and snow.

It is important to have the right size of hood for whatever lens you are using. A lens hood that is made for a standard lens will not be suitable for use with a wide angle or telephoto lens, and in some cases may cause 'vignetting', when the corners of the negative are cut off because the lens hood is not of the correct size. Most lens hoods are made of metal, but some are made of rubber and are collapsible, so can be left permanently around the lens; this can be very useful, especially, as is sometimes the case, when you are in a hurry to get a particular shot.

Tripods

Tripods are extremely useful for work in places where the light is not very good and you have to use slow shutter speeds (which can cause camera shake if the camera is hand-held). This is sometimes the case in a large station with an overall roof, but even more so inside locomotive depots or sheds. Tripods are also very useful with very long telephoto lenses, which even when used with fairly fast shutter speeds are difficult to hold steadily by hand, and again camera shake may occur.

The camera is mounted on the tripod and the shutter is fired by a cable release. When the camera is on the tripod it can be moved from side to side and up and down by a handle on the top of the tripod. Although the camera is mounted horizontally on the tripod, the tripod head can be swivelled to get the camera into the vertical position if required. The tripod's legs can also be adjusted to obtain the height at which you require the camera to be set.

The main thing to look for when buying a tripod is that it is of fairly sturdy construction, will not collapse, and is easy to erect and fold away. However, at the same time try not to get one that is too heavy, especially if you plan to take it with you on overseas trips. Tripods are also used for time exposures in night photography (see Chapter 7).

Two other pieces of equipment that the railway photographer might find of use are the monopod and gunpod. The monopod has just one adjustable leg that is balanced on a firm surface and held by hand; the shutter is usually fired by a cable release. The gunpod fits into the shoulder like a rifle, the camera is mounted on the end of it, and the shutter is fired by a trigger on the gunpod connected to the camera. Both of these pieces of equipment are useful, especially when using long telephoto lenses.

Exposure meters

Today most cameras, especially in the 35mm format, are fitted with exposure or light meters that work either automatically or manually. An automatic metering system usually has either an aperture priority system or a shutter priority system. Before using any light meter, whether built into your camera or separate, always make sure that the speed of the film you are using (its ASA number) has been correctly set on the meter.

With an aperture priority system, the lens aperture is set to the required aperture and the shutter is then automatically set by the meter, and vice versa with the shutter priority system. The latter system, where the shutter speed is controlled, is probably more useful for railway photography, especially for action work where a fast shutter speed (unless you are panning) is essential for good sharp pictures of moving trains. Some cameras are fully automatic, with both aperture and shutter being set by the meter. However, these types of cameras, like the first two, sometimes have a manual override, enabling the exposure to be adjusted.

Another system, which is probably the most useful for railway photography, has the exposure meter built into the camera but is not in any way automatic. In the case of the single lens reflex camera, it is pointed at the subject to be photographed and the meter takes the light reading through the lens. The results are shown in the camera viewfinder, letting you know whether you have the correct exposure or are under- or over-exposed (in which case adjustment of the aperture and/or shutter may be necessary until the correct exposure is obtained).

The manual metering system on a viewfinder camera takes its light reading from a window on the front of the camera, which is then transmitted to a dial, usually on the top of the camera, from where the exposure can be read and the camera adjusted accordingly.

The metering system on the twin lens camera is similar to the viewfinder camera; a window or grille is located on the front of the camera through which the meter takes its reading, but it is usually transferred to a dial on the side of the camera, from where an exposure reading is obtained. Clearly, in all these cases the camera must be pointed at the subject to be taken to obtain a correct exposure.

The great advantage with the manual system is that it is easy to adjust the exposure when photographing in difficult lighting conditions. An example is photography against the light (back lighting). The main subject may be

The problems of exposure and, consequently, the correct use of a light meter are well illustrated in these next two pictures.

In the first, which shows Brush Type 4 diesel No 47478 on a Bristol-Birmingham train passing through Birmingham University station on 8 December 1981, the snow, coupled with the side light, played havoc with the exposure meter. The exposure reading for the whole scene at 1/500th sec was f11, which would have completely underexposed the front end of the locomotive and the shadow areas, for which the meter reading was f4.5 With a balance of the two readings, and taking the scene at 1/500th sec at f6.3, I was able to produce a negative with good detail in the shadow areas. At the printing stage the overexposed sections were compensated by burning in, and the underexposed by holding back.

Camera: Nikon FM with 85mm lens plus yellow filter. Exposure: 1/500th sec at f6.3. Film: Ilford XP1 rated at 400 ASA, developed in XP1 chemicals.

very bright, which means that with a shutter speed of 1/500th sec the lens aperture needs to be closed down to f11, but the shadow area gives a reading of 1/500th sec at f4, so to get a balanced exposure with some detail in the shadow area an exposure of 1/500th sec at f6.3 or f8 would need to be used. These sorts of exposure problems are reasonably easy with a manual camera, but could be very tricky with an automatic camera.

Finally, if your camera is not fitted with any sort of light meter, you can use a separate one, a method still favoured by many professional photographers. Simply hold the meter towards the subject, take the reading and transfer it to your camera. However, whether built-in or separate, meters need to be used with care to ensure that any extraneous bright light source near the main subject is not exercising too great an influence on the meter. Equally, darker areas such as track and ballast might influence the meter the other way. Thus it is essential to check the light readings above and below the main subject to assess the

This second picture shows Class 5 4-6-0 No 45042 leaving Llandudno Junction with an evening Holyhead-Broad Street goods on 7 September 1966. The exposure problem in this picture is one of extremely contrasty back lighting. An exposure reading was made for the grass bank on the right, leaving the shiny rails to add interest to the black shadows, and at the printing stage the highlight areas were burned in. If a reading had been used based the shadow area, it would have resulted in a very washed-out effect with extreme over-exposure in the highlight regions, which would have made it an extremely difficult negative to print.

Camera: Konica range-finder with 45mm lens plus yellow filter. Exposure: 1/250th sec at f5-6. Film: Kodak Plus X rated at 125 ASA, developed in D 76 (undiluted).

overall light range and reach a decision about what level the exposure must be to bring out the detail in the principal part of the subject. For example, except in low sun, under-footplate details of a steam locomotive close to will usually be darker than the boiler top.

2
Monochrome darkroom work

While great pleasure is to be derived from taking photographs, whether it be on the lineside or in a station or shed, for many people the pleasure of developing the film and printing the negatives is just as great, for it is here in the darkroom that you are able to compose and create a little magic. At one time people tended to be put off by the mystique of darkroom work, thinking that it was extremely complicated. But today, with all the modern equipment and techniques, this is not the case and it can be enjoyed by all.

The darkroom

The essential requirements of any darkroom, whether it be a kitchen, bathroom, bedroom or a permanent room, are that it should be light-tight, have good ventilation and heating, and have access to running water. Space permitting, it is advisable to have both a wet and a dry bench, perhaps on opposite sides of the room. The reason for this is to avoid putting down negatives and papers, etc, on wet areas, something that may cause permanent damage to them.

To process a film we need the following basic equipment in the darkroom:

Developing tank
Funnel
Measuring cylinders
Thermometer
Timer
Non-fluffy cloth

The last four items are also used in printing and enlarging, together with the following equipment:

Four developing dishes or trays
Enlarger, complete with lens
Masking frame
Safelight
Three print forceps or tongs

The most important item of this equipment is the enlarger. Do not skimp on this, but buy the best that you can afford.

Make sure the enlarger is well constructed and has a column long enough to enable you to enlarge up to 15in x 12in on the baseboard. It is also very important for the negative holder to hold the film flat during exposure and not scratch it. Also make sure that the enlarger lens is of good quality, at least as good as that on the camera. So many people have excellent lenses on their cameras, but when it comes to enlargers they very often use lenses of poor quality and fail to understand why they cannot produce quality prints. It is also worth buying an enlarger with a filter drawer, thus enabling you to do colour work.

Developing a negative

It is a fairly simple job to develop a black and white film, for once a developing tank has been loaded in the darkroom the processing can then be done in daylight. But before you process your first film it is important to practise loading a film on to the spiral of the developing tank. For this purpose we can use a roll of old unimportant exposed film. First, practise loading in the light, then, when you feel confident, try it in total darkness. It may take a little time at first to acquire the knack, but with practice it should not take too long.

The first step in processing a film is to prepare the chemicals – developer, fixer, stop bath – to the required temperatures. Then *in complete darkness* (first making sure that your hands are thoroughly dry) remove the film from its roll or cassette and load it on to the spiral of the developing tank. Place the loaded spiral in the tank and replace the lid on the tank, making sure it is securely fitted.

Processing can then be done in daylight as follows. *First check to make sure that the processing chemicals are at the correct temperature.* This can be done by immersing the cylinders containing the chemicals in either hot or cold water baths in order to raise or lower the temperature to the required level. Always wipe the thermometer with the cloth after testing one cylinder of chemical, to avoid carrying over drops and contaminating another cylinder.

Next pour the developer into the tank through the opening in the lid and give the spiral several quick twists to dislodge any air bubbles, then agitate according to the manufacturer's instructions for the type of developer you are using. Remember that the development time starts as soon as the developer is poured into the tank.

When the development time is up, tip out the developer (keeping the lid on) and pour in the stop bath (which should be at the same temperature as the developer) and agitate for 30 seconds or so. Pour out the stop bath and pour in the fixer, which once again should be at the same temperature as the developer and stop bath. Agitate for the first 30 to 60 seconds, then every 30 seconds during the stated fixing time. After the film has been in the fixer for at least a minute, you can then lift the lid off the tank and inspect the outer frames of the film, but do *not* unwind the film from the spiral because it is almost impossible to rewind a wet film back on to a spiral. When the film has been fixed it is far easier to wash it in the developing tank.

Washing is very important, and a sudden change of temperature from the development temperature of, say, 68° will cause reticulation or coarse grain. The way to avoid this is gradually to bring down the temperature in the tank to that of the tap water. Do this by constantly changing the water in the tank and lowering the temperature slightly each time. Once you arrive at tap water temperature you will be able to wash the film under the tap. Do this by using a rubber hose and direct the water down into the bottom of the tank. The water will then come back up the side of the tank, washing the whole of the film. Wash for around 30 to 45 minutes. At the end of the wash add a few drops of wetting agent to the tank water, which helps the water to run off the film and avoids staining. After washing, remove the film from the spiral and hang it up to dry in a dust-free room, attaching a clip to the bottom of the film to prevent it curling up. Some people advocate the use of a squeegee to remove surplus water, but in practice this can sometimes scratch the emulsion. Instead it may be safer to use a damp soft brush, oxhair or sable, to blot off surplus water, froth from the wetting agent, or specks of dust. Once the film has dried, cut it into strips of six (35mm) or four (6 x 6cm) ready for storage (see Chapter 9).

Recommended film-developer combinations

These combination are all at a temperature of 68°F/20°C.

Ilford FP4 and Aculux, rated at 160 ASA: Development times are 6½ minutes for 35mm and 8½ minutes for 120 roll film. This combination gives fine grain and very good contrast. Dilution is 1+9.

Ilford Pan F and ID11, rated at 50 ASA: Use developer undiluted and develop for 6 minutes for both 35mm and 120 sizes. Gives very fine grain and resolution.

Kodak Plus X and D76, Ilford FP4 and ID11, both rated at 125 ASA: Development time for both combinations is 6½ minutes using undiluted developer. These are standard combinations giving good sharpness, grain and contrast. Developer times are the same for both 35mm and 120 roll film.

Kodak Tri-X and D76, rated at 400 ASA: The development time for both 35mm and 120 sizes using undiluted developer is 8 minutes. This is another popular combination giving good results, especially with the 120 size film.

Ilford FP4 and Acuspecial, rated at 200 ASA: The dilution for this is 1+29 for 35mm and 1+19 for 120 size. Development time for both sizes is 14 minutes. This combination gives very good fine detail and contrast resulting in a noticeable increase in apparent sharpness, and is at its best in high contrast conditions. It requires very careful development.

Although this developer can be used with 120 roll film, it is particularly suitable for 35mm work, especially when used with good-quality cameras and enlarging equipment.

Printing and enlarging

Having developed the negatives, the next step is to make prints from them. Before you start to enlarge the negatives, it is very useful to make contact prints, enabling you to select the best pictures for enlarging and saving you hours of unnecessary work and wasted materials.

First, set out the chemicals in dishes in the following order:

1 Developer
2 Stop bath
3 Fixer
4 Water

Temperatures are not as critical as when processing films, but it is better to keep all the chemicals at around 68°F/20°C.

Contact strips can be made in the following two ways:

Contact printing frame: Place the strips of film into the contact frame, then, by the light of a safelight only, place a sheet of 8in x 10in printing paper (grade 2) into the printer and close.

Plate glass: With only the safelight on, place the negatives, shiny side up, on top of a piece of 8in x 10in printing paper (grade 2). Then place a sheet of plate glass (the same size as the printing paper) on top of the negatives. Make sure the glass has been thoroughly cleaned beforehand to avoid marking the negatives.

Whichever method you chose to use, exposure is the same for both, either by switching the room light on for 2 or 3 seconds or by what is perhaps a more accurate method, using the enlarger. Place the unit on the enlarger baseboard and, with the lens at full aperture and at least 2 feet from the baseboard, expose for 2 or 3 seconds. Remove the paper from the unit or glass and proceed to develop the contact sheet, using the same process as for general printing, a process described in detail later in this section.

Before describing the enlarging process, let us look at the main types of negatives from which you will be making prints. In theory, if you have exposed and developed your film correctly you should only need to print the negatives on normal paper (grade 2). However, in practice it is a different matter. Subjects can be flat or contrasting. Exposures may be wrong because of lighting, etc. We may over-develop or under-develop the film, and so on. With this in mind, illustrated on pages 26-27 are the most common negative types that you will encounter, as follows:

Soft, flat negative, lacking contrast: This is usually caused by under-exposure and/or under -development.

Harsh, contrasty negative: This type of negative is generally caused by over-exposure and/or over-development.

Normal negative: There is good detail in both the dark (highlight) and light (shadow) areas.

Beside each negative is a print made on three different grades of paper (printing paper can be obtained in various grades from soft through to hard – grades 1 to 3 or 4). It will be seen that the soft negative prints well on hard paper – grade 3; the contrasty negative prints well on soft paper – grade 1; and the normal negative is correctly printed on normal paper – grade 2. As well as keeping the normal grade of paper in stock, it is advisable to have some of the other grades to hand.

Having set out the chemicals (the same as for contact printing), place the strip of negatives in the enlarger, shiny side up and back to front; this is because when the negative is projected on to the baseboard it will appear the other way round. Before inserting the negatives into the enlarger, it is very important to remove dust particles with a small brush.

Switch on the safelight and switch off the room light – do not switch on the room light again until the print is fixed.

Switch on the enlarger, making sure that the lens is at full aperture (wide open). Raise the enlarger head until the negative is framed on the masking frame at the required size. Focus the negative, making absolutely sure that it is sharply focused. Then inspect the image and decide what grade of paper is required. Once that is decided, stop the lens down by two stops (to increase the depth of focus) and switch off the enlarger.

As it is very difficult to make a perfect print first time, it is wise to make a test print. Place a sheet of the correct grade of printing paper in the masking frame (remembering to close the packet of unexposed paper), then expose for 2 to 5 seconds, depending on the size of the enlargement. Now cover a small section of the print (say a fifth) with a piece of card and expose again for the same amount of time as the first exposure. Repeat this until you have covered the paper completely. By now you should have five test exposures that are multiples of the first exposure, eg 2, 4, 6, 8, 10 seconds.

Next slide the exposed test prints into the developer and agitate by rocking the dish. After 1-3 minutes (depending on the type of paper you are using – resin-coated papers require around 1-2 minutes in development, and conventional bromide papers between 1½ and 3 minutes) lift out the print with the developer tongs and place it in the stop bath – without getting the tongs in the stop bath – then put the tongs back on the side of the developing dish. After agitating for 20 seconds or so remove the print from the stop bath using the stop bath tongs (not the ones used with the developer) and place it in the fixer, again without getting the stop bath tongs in the fixer. Agitate for 30 seconds or so, then turn on the room light and inspect the test print, from which you should now be able to judge the correct exposure time for that particular negative.

Turn off the room light again and check to make sure that the negative is still in focus. Now you are ready to make the final print, which is processed in exactly the same way as the test print, but given the correct exposure time. It is important to develop the print fully and never snatch it out of the developer too early. After the print has been fixed for the required time, using the fixer tongs place it in the dish of water in readiness for washing later on; do not put the tongs of one dish into the chemical for the next part of the process, otherwise drops of chemical will be transferred back. If you are using resin-coated paper, washing only takes around 5 minutes. Just place the dish of prints under a running tap – tepid water if possible – and separate them continuously for 5 minutes. After washing, remove surplus water with photographic blotting paper and leave to dry, or alternatively dry with a hair-dryer.

Soft flat negative

Grade 3 paper (hard)

Harsh, contrasty negative

Grade 1 paper (soft)

Normal negative

Grade 2 paper (normal)

Normal paper

Soft paper

Normal paper

Hard paper

Soft paper

Hard paper

A typical 35mm contact sheet printed on a piece of 10in x 8in printing paper. (Both the 15 exposures of the 645 format and the 12 exposures of the 6 x 6cm format fit exactly on a 10in x 8in sheet, but for the 10 exposures of the 6 x 7cm size it is necessary to use a 10in x 12in sheet of printing paper.)

Right A test print of picture 17 on the contact sheet (third from the left on the third line) and the final print, showing 'A4' 'Pacific' No 4498 pulling out of Grange-over-Sands with the southbound 'Cumbrian Coast Express' on 22 August 1978. It will be seen that the exposure for the final print is around 3 seconds for the foreground and train (allowing for detail in the shadow area) and around 5 seconds for the background and sky. On bigger enlargements the exposures for the test print would obviously be longer, for example 4, 8, 12, 16, 20 seconds, etc.

Camera: Nikkormat with 135mm lens plus yellow filter.
Exposure: 1/250th sec at f4. Film: Ilford Pan F rated at 50 ASA, developed in ID11 undiluted.

Conventional bromide paper prints take between 30 and 45 minutes to wash. They can either be washed in a special print washer or by changing the water in the dish every 5 minutes and at the same time separating the prints once or twice. Repeat this process for up to 45 minutes, by which time the prints should be thoroughly washed. After washing, remove any surplus water with photographic blotting paper and leave to dry, or dry them on a flat-bed dryer.

Summary of the printing process

1 Prepare chemicals to around 68°F/20°C.
2 Clean the negative and insert into the enlarger.
3 Switch on the safelight and switch off the room light.
4 Switch on the enlarger and raise the head to enlarge the negative to the required size. Focus the negative.
5 Inspect the negative to decide which grade of printing paper is to be used.
6 Stop down the lens by two stops and switch off the enlarger.
7 Remove the printing paper from its packet (sealing the packet afterwards) and place it in the masking frame, emulsion side up.
8 Make the exposures for a test strip.
9 Develop for 1-3 minutes.
10 Stop bath.
11 Fixer.
12 Switch on the room light and examine the print to determine the correct exposure and make sure that the grade of paper is correct.
13 Switch off the room light and make the final print.
14 Wash and dry the print.

Never allow daylight or room light to fall on unexposed printing paper or it will become fogged.

Glazing

One of the advantages of using resin-coated gloss paper is that when the print has been dried it has a very high glaze, but with conventional bromide gloss paper it is necessary to glaze the print to achieve the same high gloss.

To glaze prints we need a chrome glazing sheet large enough to take two or more prints, a rubber roller and if possible a flat-bed dryer. The glazing process is as follows:

1 Turn on the dryer to the recommended setting for glaze.
2 Clean the glazing sheet with a clean damp cloth, then polish it with a dry soft cloth.
3 Place the wet prints face down on the glazing sheet and use the rubber roller, working from the centre outwards, to push out any excess water from beneath

the prints. Use blotting paper to mop up the excess water.

4 Place the glazing sheet (with the prints on top) on the dryer, which by now should be at the correct temperature. Bring the canvas top of the dryer down over the prints and secure.
5 Leave for 10-15 minutes, then remove the canvas top of the dryer, by which time the prints should be glazed and will pop off the glazing sheet. If they do not, in no circumstances must you force them off as this will cause blemishes in the glaze. Instead, close the canvas top of the glazer again and leave the prints for a few more minutes. If they do not pop off this time it may be because the dryer is not warm enough. If this is the case swab the prints with hot water to remove them from the glazing sheet and start the glazing process again when the dryer has heated up.

It is not necessary to use a dryer to glaze your prints. Once the prints have been mounted on the glazing sheet and the excess water removed, simply leave them to dry and after an hour or so they should pop off the glazing sheet fully glazed. Obviously this method takes a great deal longer to glaze a batch of prints.

Spotting

It is very difficult to produce a print that is entirely free from blemishes in conditions outside a laboratory. To help the amateur, here is a list of the marks you will frequently meet, with some suggestions on how to correct them. All restoration work is easier on the print than on the negative because of the size, and it is better not to tamper with the original.

The following equipment will be needed: a very fine brush, preferably size 00 sable hair; a white saucer and water, and a clean rag; good even lighting; either a stain such as 'Spotone', which penetrates to the paper, or an ink, which lies on the surface of the paper; and a white pigment such as 'Process White'. Also useful are a sharp blade for 'knifing', a bleach such as 'Spotoff', and finally – patience.

The usual blemish is the white spot or white hair, caused by dust lying on the surface of the paper during exposure, or lying on the negative. Dust often sticks to the negative when it is hanging up to dry, so a draught-free room is useful to avoid this. Static also attracts dust to these surfaces, so try not to wear synthetic clothing that crackles in the dark.

White marks are easier to hide in a textured background such as trees, and difficult in pale featureless skies. If using a stain, dilute it to a paler shade and stipple a very small amount with the tip of the brush, which should be damp, but not dripping. Let this dry first as it will darken, then apply more if needed. If using an ink, remember that this

Above The upper picture of rebuilt 'West Country' 'Pacific' No 34036 *Westward Ho* at speed near Basing with a down Bournemouth train on 8 April 1966 is now history, but is completely spoiled by the telegraph pole sticking out of the smokebox; other blemishes are a black spot in the exhaust and several white spots in the sky above.

Right This picture shows the restoration work complete with the pole bleached out with 'Spotoff'. This compound comes in two parts, mixed in proportion according to the control of speed required. After the print has been completely washed, apply the compound to the wet print until the bleaching out is complete. Then the print is washed briefly and re-fixed for around a minute. Wash the print again and dry it, then retouch the white area remaining with dilute stains to match the surrounds. If using glossy paper *do not* glaze the print until this final bleaching is complete.

This process is useful for salvaging historic photographs and modern scenes when, for example, someone stands in the shot at the last minute. However, prevention at the time the picture is taken is always better than cure!

Camera: Konica range-finder with 45mm fixed lens plus yellow filter. Exposure: 1/500th sec at 15-6. Film: Kodak Plus X, developed in D76 (undiluted).

lies on the surface, and as it dries it tends to leave a 'halo' of darker ink. Anticipate this by using a lighter tone, first diluting the ink in a saucer; when it is dry, touch up the paler centre of the halo with a little more ink. Resin-coated papers are tricky as the ink tends to blob; a binder such as a little pigment mixed with the ink is helpful. Scratches from wiping the water off the negative are usually white and very fine; they need more practice to correct.

Another blemish is the black mark from a tear in the negative. If it is small it is easy to nick it out of the paper with a sharp blade, and reglaze the spot with a little gum arabic such as 'Gloy'. If it is a large mark, it is better to bleach it out, and stipple in the white area with stains until the patch blends with the background. This technique can be used to obliterate the odd 'gricer' – the unthinking enthusiast – who rushes up at the last minute into your shot!

Other blemishes are not so simple, and need covering with a white or blended pigment. Iron marks, those small brown craters in the surface, are found in some parts of the country, arising from the water supply. Another mark is the grey 'bruise' from rough handling with tongs in the developing bath. The remedy is prevention. A darker grey ring in the middle of your print is perhaps the most difficult to cover up, and is caused by the filament of the bulb in your enlarger. Check that you have the right bulb, and that all the pieces of your enlarger are in place. Ordinary light bulbs are unsuitable because of the bulb details printed across the glass.

With the advent of modern technology, an alternative to the manual method of spotting just described is to scan the print digitally and enhance it on the computer screen, as described in Chapter 1.

Shading and dodging

Shading and dodging simply means giving different exposures to different areas of the negative. This is very relevant to railway photography, for it would be fair to say that the great majority of railway photographs need a certain amount of shading and dodging, some to a far greater degree than others.

There are two main reasons for this. The first is the need to show good details in the sky, an important feature when photographing any kind of traction, but especially important when photographing a heavy exhaust (which is invariably set against the sky) from a steam engine, or sometimes from a diesel. This can turn an ordinary picture into something very exciting, conveying the power and strength of the locomotive. To some extent the sky and exhaust can be brought out more on the negative by the use of filters (see the previous chapter). Nevertheless, even

when using a filter the sky and exhaust usually require more exposure at the printing stage than the main body of the negative.

The second important point (often forgotten) is the foreground. In railway photographs the foreground frequently consists of station platforms, track ballast, grass verges and banks. As we usually expose for the main scene – the train – the foreground, like the sky and exhaust, tends to be a little over-exposed and needs extra exposure at the printing stage. It is very important to have good strong foreground tones, even perhaps a little on the dark side to focus attention on the main subject.

There are two methods of shading, by using your hands, a technique used by professional printers, or by using a dodging and shading kit, which can either be bought at photographic stores or made at home.

Using your hands to shade can be tricky and you may find it easier to use a set of home-made shaders and dodgers. This consists of two pieces of 10in x 8in card (which covers all prints up to 10in x 8in in size), one of them plain and the other having a hole about 1 inch across cut into it roughly off centre. The other dodger consists of a small round piece of card about three-quarters of an inch across, attached to a piece of wire 8 inches in length. You will find that these usually cover any contingency

Most railway pictures will require extra exposure in the sky and foreground and this can be achieved by 'burning in' these parts. After developing the test print, check the sky and foreground and you will usually find that to get an equal balance of tones all over the picture more exposure will need to be given to either one or both of these than to the main body of the picture. This is where the first of our home-made shaders comes in – the 10in x 8in piece of plain card. After exposing the print for the correct time for the main picture, switch off the enlarger, then hold the 10in x 8in card about 3-4 inches above the paper (to increase the shadow area), covering everything except the sky.

Figure 4: Shaders and dodgers

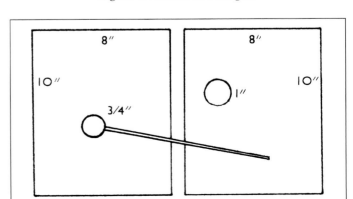

Switch on the enlarger and expose for the correct time for the sky, but at the same time keep the card moving slightly to prevent a line appearing on the finished print where you have shaded in. Now switch off the enlarger again, and if necessary repeat the process, but this time giving extra exposure to the foreground. The print can then be processed in the normal way. Be very careful when shading to avoid knocking the enlarger, which will cause vibrations and ruin the print.

The technique of using the other dodgers is similar. The 10in x 8in card with the small hole in it is used to burn in small things like buffer beams, locomotive numbers, reporting numbers and the like. If the section to be burned in is on the edge of the picture, raise the card towards the enlarger head, which increases the shadow size, thus enabling you to move the card off centre and still cover the main part of the picture. The small circular card on the wire is used to hold back smaller details, especially the front ends of locomotives (when the photograph is taken against back lighting), wheels and any other smaller items that need less exposure than the main picture.

At first you will find it difficult to shade and dodge prints, but in time and with perseverance most people achieve a fair degree of success. It is worthwhile keeping your early efforts at shading and, after a period of time, make a comparison with your current work. You should be very pleasantly surprised.

Double printing

Double printing requires much care and attention to achieve reasonable results, but can be very useful in railway photography.

For example, you may have a good sharp negative of a rare steam locomotive at work, but because the photograph was taken on a very warm summer's day no exhaust is showing. By double printing we can add the exhaust from another negative and bring the original picture to life.

A word of caution – this technique is usually only successful when the locomotive is set against the sky, since it is more or less impossible to double print against a background of anything else.

The technique for double printing is as follows:

1 Take a piece of card the same size as the print required and place it in the masking frame on the enlarger baseboard.
2 Place the negative of the train in the enlarger and expose it on to the card, then, having focused, etc, draw the outline of the train and the horizon on the card. Switch off the enlarger.

3 Remove the card from the masking frame and, by cutting round the outline of the train and horizon, divide the card into two masks, marking them 'top' and 'bottom'.
4 Place the printing paper into the masking frame and swing the red filter into position (to cover the lens), then turn on the enlarger.
5 Place the top mask round the top of the train and horizon so that the sky is covered. Uncover the lens by moving the red filter and make an exposure, then switch off the enlarger.
6 Once again swing the red filter into position and turn on the enlarger. Remove the top mask and replace it with the bottom mask, which covers the train and landscape. Switch off the enlarger.
7 Remove the negative of the train and replace it with the negative of the exhaust to be printed in.
8 Swing the red filter into position and turn on the enlarger.
9 Line up the exhaust with the chimney of the locomotive, making sure that the exhaust is in focus.
10 Uncover the lens by moving the red filter and make an exposure, then process the print as normal.

It is very important to place the masks correctly or you will finish up with an obvious join.

Double printing is a very skilful process, so expect quite a few failures before success is achieved.

Composing on the enlarger baseboard

Developing and printing the negative has almost as much magic about it as being out on the lineside. Today, even after many years of railway photography, I never cease to be thrilled at being able to capture on film that split-second of action. And after a day filming I am always eager to develop the film, usually the same night if possible or at the very latest by the next day, then printing the negative as soon as possible after that.

When you are out photographing you compose your pictures in the viewfinder, and after developing the film you generally print the negative more or less as it is. But there are quite a few occasions when you can do some composition work, often quite radical, on the enlarger baseboard.

Once you have the negative in the enlarger, focused and ready to print, look carefully at the composition, because it may be that by some fairly simple adjustments you can alter this with startling results.

One very simple thing that you can do is to change the format of the picture from horizontal to vertical or vice versa. To do this you may need to enlarge or decrease the picture size accordingly. Many photographs have started life as horizontals and finished up as vertical compositions. Never be afraid to crop your pictures. When you inspect the pictures on the baseboard keep a large piece of card handy and use it to cover different portions of the picture. Your picture may look flat at 10in x 8in, but may come alive cropped down to, say, 10in x 5in. Look at the many fine pictures in books and magazines that are not of conventional sizes.

Be prepared to experiment with your compositions and you will find that this adds another enjoyable and satisfying dimension to darkroom work.

Print quality

Once you have mastered the technique of developing a monochrome print and are able to produce a reasonable photograph, it is very important to concentrate on producing a first-class print.

A top-quality print is one that contains a good range of tones from black through to white, with plenty of detail in the shadow areas and, above all, one that is sharp all over. For this you obviously require a good sharp negative with an average amount of contrast and good detail throughout. You can achieve reasonable prints from negatives that lack some of these requirements (with the obvious exception of

These two pictures well illustrate baseboard composition. Class 9F 2-10-0 *Evening Star* is seen at speed near Micklefield with the morning York Circular train on 9 July 1978. The 'landscape' format picture is a print of the whole of the negative, which as it stands is obviously not very satisfactory from a composition point of view. By drastic cropping we finish up with the second 'portrait' format picture, which gives us a much more satisfactory composition because the centre of interest (the front end of the train) falls on the Golden Section (see Chapter 5) and also has curved lines (rails and exhaust) leading to that point.

Another frame was shot after this one in which the train was balanced up with the signal box on the left, which meant that I was able to obtain two satisfactory pictures.

It will be noted that the finished print is only 2/5ths of the original negative, which ably demonstrates the quality of today's better 35mm lenses and cameras, especially when used with fine grain film like Ilford Pan F.

Camera: Nikkormat with 50mm standard lens plus yellow filter. Exposure: 1/500th sec at f4. Film: Ilford Pan F rated at 50 ASA, developed in ID11 (undiluted).

sharpness), but generally to achieve a top-quality print you need a first-class negative.

Provided that they are careful and consistent during processing, most photographers, after a certain period of trial and error, will begin to produce good negatives. There

will always be the negative that because of lighting conditions or miscalculation is not quite up to standard, but if you take care they should not be too numerous.

Thus, assuming that we have developed a roll of film to the required standard and made a contact sheet, before we start to enlarge and print the negatives we must do two very important things: inspect the contact sheet and pick out the best compositions, then look at the corresponding negatives and place them in order of difficulty, beginning with the one that you think will be the easiest to print and finishing with the most difficult.

At first you may find this difficult to do, but you can take it as a general guide that a negative with a good tonal range, fairly even lighting and a small amount of shadow area is usually easier to print than one taken with back lighting and therefore with plenty of shadows and contrast, if only because as a rule less shading and dodging is required with the first type of negative. Always start with the easiest negative because once you have a couple of prints processed to your satisfaction it is then easier psychologically to tackle the more difficult ones.

Having selected your negative, placed it in the enlarger (remembering to remove any dust and hair), and brought it to the required size on the baseboard, take great care over the focusing, checking that it is pin-sharp all over. Sometimes the enlarger head may be slightly out of alignment causing one edge to be out of focus. The foam on the bottom of the masking frame may be worn at one side and this may cause focusing problems. It is important to check all these things to ensure picture sharpness. Using a glassless negative carrier in the enlarger can also be a cause of lack of sharpness because of the popping of negatives as they warm up; this is particularly so when using the larger negative sizes. Always check the focus before every exposure (remembering to stop the lens down again once this has been done).

Always make a test print – this will save you time and materials as well as being a vital factor in the achievement of a first-rate print.

Never under-develop your print – always allow full development time and a little extra if necessary. This is essential to obtain a full range of tones. Experience will tell you when a print is ready to be removed from the developer. A point worth noting is that a print will darken slightly when it is dried, so if it appears a little on the light side when being washed it may be all right once it has been dried.

It is always very important to wash prints for at least the required time to ensure permanence. If your prints have not been washed sufficiently, after a period of possibly months or even years stains will begin to appear and ruin the print. This also applies if they have not been fixed for the correct amount of time, in which case they will begin to turn brown, once again ruining them and of course wasting hours of work and materials. It is also essential that you should be as clean and tidy as possible in your darkroom, ensuring that the enlarging equipment is regularly dusted and cleaned, particularly before use, and that all processing equipment is thoroughly washed before and after use.

All these factors should help towards high-quality printing, but in addition it is important to study other photographers' work, especially at exhibitions, etc. It is here that you should be able to see what a top-class print really looks like and make comparisons with your own work.

Mounting and presentation

For home use (as described in Chapter 9) you may wish to keep your prints in albums, but for exhibition work you will need a more formal presentation, mounting individual photographs on card mounts like pictures. The white edge left by some masking frames should always be trimmed off squarely, using either a blade and ruler or a rotary trimmer.

The mounting card should be thick, matt-surfaced, and of a colour that will not detract from the photograph. Some people prefer white, some black and others prefer a neutral tone such as elephant or donkey. Black and white prints are better on a shade with little colour, while colour prints can stand a hue such as puce, evergreen or slate.

The size and placing are also matters of choice. If the print is small and historic, it would benefit from a large mount. If the print is very large, the mount could be trimmed to match the edges – 'block mounting'. Some people prefer an even width of border, others mount the print slightly higher than centre. However, if you are displaying a set of prints you must be consistent.

These are two ways of fixing the photograph on the card, either by glue or by adhesive sheets. Glues come in liquid form or in aerosol sprays or adhesive sticks. Some rely on the solvent drying out, while some need heat to melt the contacts.

The important things to watch for are that the glue does not spread in ridges, that the solvent has time to evaporate before pressing the print down – very important with resin-coated papers – that you can have a second chance to position the prints, and that you can remove any blobs of glue at the edges. It is always best to mark in at least one edge with a fine pencil line on the card to guide your placement, making sure that it is square with the edges.

Aerosols such as Scotch Photo Mount have adjustable spray widths for economy, allow for repositioning, and become permanent after 10 minutes. Cover your worktable with rough paper and spray both surfaces to be glued, using a mask of scrap paper over the area of card that will show. Position the print and rub down with a soft cloth, working from the centre outwards to avoid trapping air bubbles. A stick adhesive such as Pritt looks like a giant lip-salve. Wipe the stick over both surfaces, masking the card, etc. This method is handy for small prints.

Spread-on glues such as Cow Gum need a very thin coating on both surfaces, using a wide-edged spreader to avoid ridges. Protect your table with rough paper, apply the adhesive thinly and give it a few minutes for the solvent fumes to evaporate, then position and rub down from the centre. Any smears of glue can be rubbed off with a clean rag.

Rubber solution glues such as Copydex are used in much the same way, being careful when spreading not to touch any dry glue that will pull in rubbery threads. Positioning has to be right first time for this.

Patersons produce a Thermal Print Mountant in liquid form, which is applied with a brush to both surfaces and left to dry for half an hour. When the print has been positioned, cover it with a clean sheet of paper and press it down with an iron on a cool to medium heat setting. This is safe with resin-coated papers. Dry Mounting Tissue also uses heat to stick the print down. The sheet of tissue should not project beyond the edge of the photograph, and the easiest way to make sure of this is to start with an untrimmed print. Lay the tissue on the back of the photograph and hold it in place with a few dabs from the tip of a hot iron, then trim both together. If your print is already trimmed, tack down the tissue with the iron and trim away the surplus with a blade. Position the print on the card, protect with paper and press with a medium hot iron – it is best to experiment on scraps, particularly with resin-coated papers. If the tissue does not quite stick to the card, apply more heat; if the tissue sticks to the card, but the print comes away, iron again using a lower setting.

The finished mount looks good when left perfectly plain, but some like to frame the photo with a single line, about a centimetre from the edges. If you use ink, rule the lines with a fountain pen or ruling pen with a width adjustment. Draw a pencil line as a guide, then turn your ruler over to prevent ink from creeping under the edge. It is better to use less ink and go over the line again. Always test on a spare piece of card before you work on the actual mount.

If you are exhibiting, write your name, title and description of the photograph on the back, for the benefit of those compiling the catalogue. If you want the title to appear on the front, you can draw directly on to the card freehand or using a stencil, or you can apply transfer letters for a professional finish.

3
Colour photography

The most satisfying composition in colour will have the same 'skeleton' as a black and white picture, for it will rely on a structure that has lines or connections directing your eyes to the focus of interest. It will have balance of detail and balance in the placing of light and dark, but with the added ingredient of placing a strong colour against a subdued colour. It will also have interesting patterns or surface details. Without these, your picture will be just an ordinary snapshot and never make the front cover of a magazine. Speaking of magazines, we owe a lot to the colour supplements of several Sunday newspapers, which have done so much to open our eyes to colour and pattern in unexpected places. The newspaper photographers are really artists who have taught us by their skill in composition to see the world in a fresh light. Many of their pictures still hold our attention by their underlying quality, long after their news value has faded.

It is more difficult to take a good railway colour picture on several counts, the first being that the element of colour stacks up the odds against keeping out distracting features. As already mentioned, it is much easier with black and white prints to spot out the last-minute 'gricer' who rushes into your shot by turning him into a tree! It is difficult in colour to disguise the family dressed in fluorescent anoraks who will move into the middle of the open field in your line of sight just as you are about to take an approaching steam special. Other things can get in the way, such as cars. There is no need to park right by a level crossing, when you could pull up on a verge 10 yards back, leaving the view clear. Perhaps you do want something bright in the foreground, but dozens of other photographers might not like your choice of colour.

The colours of the rainbow, or spectrum, range from visible indigo blue (ultraviolet being invisible) through greens and yellows to deepest red. White daylight is a mixture of all these, and objects reflect the parts of the spectrum that are appropriate, ie they have colours. Objects lit by only one colour, such as by signal lights or by sodium street lamps, can only appear in the colour available. In nature the blue colours we perceive tend to appear on the horizon and in the sky – in other words they are far away. Blue colours tend to fill in wide areas and form backgrounds. Blue is the colour seen best by the retina of the eye when the light is dim, as at night, and when the pupil of the eye is on wide aperture. Therefore by association, blue is a receding colour, restful and non-aggressive. Red, on the other hand, is a dominant penetrating colour, and is used to alert us to danger. Conveniently, the wavelengths of red light travel better over long distances than green or blue, which is why red is used to signal 'stop' to a train far away, and why green can be used when the locomotive is waiting for 'go' by the gantry. Reds and yellows are also sunny colours and, by association, photographs using these colours tend to have a happy feeling, whereas pictures showing much blue tend to be wistful or melancholy like a rainy day. The exception would depend on the brightness and intensity of the blue, such as an engine painted in Caledonian Blue standing in brilliant sunshine. It was one of the French Impressionists who said that 'one square metre of blue is bluer than one square centimetre'.

If you want your picture to have depth, make sure that the background is misty and has a blue or green cast, and that your subject, ie the locomotive, shows the red buffer beam, in the case of steam, or the yellow front of the cab, in the case of a diesel. When an engine is travelling at speed towards you and you want to convey this impression, this dramatic device of the bright red or yellow in the foreground never fails. The train jumps out of the picture. Indeed, on some transparencies the red is almost three-dimensional against a blue-green background. There are other things that you can use in the foreground to establish nearness. Signals are a good example, especially the red/white sides of semaphore arms, or the yellow fishtails of distant signals. Level crossing gates are another, and posts bearing numbers painted yellow. Some photographers place bunches of flowers in strategic places to liven up the scene, but conservationists would probably object most strongly! A gorse bush in full bloom would be much better, or in winter a patch of bracken.

The red/green contrast demonstrates in colour the same principle of contrast in black and white. It is a colour version of tonal recession, whereby objects of strongly contrasted light and dark stand out, and misty grey areas recede. This is a similar effect to that of focusing on a close object leaving the background a blur. Any strong contrast will stand out, for example the white lamps on the front of a black smokebox, or the black and yellow stripes on a diesel shunter. If the locomotive is rather dirty and drab, you must try to find some contrast. You might silhouette it against a light shed wall, or a brightly coloured container wagon, or even against the sky; the orange disc of the setting sun or the clouds around it make a stunning impact. On shed, you might find a worker in a new boilersuit who would be happy to pose at the chimney end. Even a pile of oil drums could be pressed into service.

Some locomotives blend into the landscape because of the colours they are painted, especially in the distance, such as *Sir Nigel Gresley*, painted Garter Blue, the preserved green 'Deltic', and Great Western locomotives. Other greens, such as that of *Lord Nelson*, tend to clash with the landscape and must be sited with care. The human eye is very sensitive to greens and can tell the difference between more similar shades than in reds. Fortunately colour films are designed to match what we see, though there may be a slight cast in one brand compared with another.

You might want to try using the theme of one colour for your photograph, instead of exploiting contrasts, and create a 'mood' picture. For this you will need to search out locations that enhance the colour of your subject. You might find *Sir Nigel Gresley* on the Cumbrian Coast route running by water on a day when the sky and sea are blue. *King George V* looks very handsome on a summer's day running up the Welsh Marches through pastures and past broad-leaved trees. The yellow nose of an HST echoes the intense yellow of fields of rape in May. *Princess Elizabeth* or *Duchess of Hamilton* could be photographed passing brick walls of factories. A 'Western' diesel, painted in the putty-coloured livery, could be found a setting by a quarry or landslip. A bright-red locomotive on the Lakeside Railway might pass by a bank of corn poppies, or that lilac colliery engine at Carnforth could one day stand by waste ground covered in purple fireweed. Even someone's washing on a clothes line might tone in with your engine. You will find many more applications of this idea of the colour theme once you start looking.

Different brands of film have slightly different colour casts. You will have to experiment to find the one you like and stick to it, especially if you intend to give slide shows, because if your magazine contains a random jumble of greenish slides or reddish slides, the effect will be disturbing. Some makes of lens are noted for their colour contrast, while others give a softer blend of colours. Your final choice of film may depend on which one suits your lens resolution, and here your photographic supplier should be able to advise you. The use of filters will also be a determining factor in the colour cast of your pictures (see page 19). When buying film for outdoor daylight use and (blue) flash photography, make sure that you get the right sort, not the film for indoor work by tungsten lamps. Indoor film will give you photographs of the outside world with a pronounced blue cast, while outdoor film used by artificial light will give you an orange cast. There are compensating filters for those interested in experimenting with these effects.

Colour films, in addition to being balanced for certain lighting conditions, are made in different speeds, marked in ASA or DIN ratings (see the Glossary). The most widely used speeds are 64 ASA for slide transparencies and 100 ASA for colour negative film. Many other speeds are available; 25 ASA is excellent in very sunny countries and gives brilliant detail, although much faster speeds for specialist applications can be obtained, but generally the faster the film, the coarser the grain.

The next aspect to consider is the quantity of light. There is usually not enough. Your train has been delayed and missed its path, it is getting dark and you are cold, and you are stuck with 64 ASA film. So you have the following choices: you could try to 'freeze' the movement of the locomotive, even on 1/125th sec, by taking it almost head-on, when the train makes very little movement across the line of vision; you could treat it as a silhouette and forget the shadow detail – this is particularly good for dawn or sunset shots on bridges; you could treat it as a 'nocturne', making sure that there are plenty of lights in cottage windows, etc; you could take the picture at a great distance, reducing the visible movement; you could set your camera on a much longer exposure and take the moving streak of light; or you could try a panned shot. It helps to have a tripod and cable release in these circumstances to ensure freedom from camera shake, especially if you are shivering! If you want to attempt the standard 'three-quarter front' shot, you will be using the widest aperture possible in order to keep the shutter speed fast. This means that the depth of field that will be in focus will be shallow. It is better to set your focus on one predetermined spot and take the best shot you can, than attempt two or three, and try to cope with winding-on and focusing at the same time, when the train is hurtling down on you at 60mph.

There are times when subdued daylight is an advantage, such as when you are photographing very shiny surfaces, or trying to show the brilliant colour of the paintwork. If the sun is very bright the colours will be lost in the intense light and shade. A light haze over the sun is very good in these circumstances, or reflected light. This can be found shining back from station walls and platforms, or from light-coloured goods wagons. The principle is the same as using a white umbrella in portrait photography. You can also create some exciting effects by looking at engines reflected in very shiny paintwork or brightly polished brass fittings, or including the colour of something just out of sight of the camera by lending its colour to the scene in the reflections. You could experiment with this idea at your leisure in a railway museum.

Exposure in these conditions depends on what you want to emphasise, either the sparkle of shiny surfaces or the colour of the groundwork. To be on the safe side you could 'bracket' the exposure by taking shots over and under the exposure that you think appropriate. Beware of the reflected image of the sun burning straight into your lens and upsetting your reading. Try to interpose some relevant object, or move slightly so that the image comes into a dull or non-reflecting area.

Reflected sunlight has its uses. When the train is late and the sun is setting, you will find that the rails shine brightly at one particular point, the 'flash point'. Aim to take your picture there, as the sun will be reflected off the locomotive like a lighthouse beam. And that glorious sight will make up for all the trials and tribulations of the day.

Most railway photographers send away their colour films to be processed. If you do, your compositions will come back exactly as you took them. If you are using colour negative film it is an easy matter to have selective enlargements made. This is also the case if you intend to make prints from slides. However, with slides that are intended primarily for projection, generally you are stuck with the picture that you took, so here are a few guides to making better pictures (which of course apply to all types of film).

First, remember that the camera takes in a little more at the edges than you see through the viewfinder, particularly if you wear glasses, preventing you from getting your eye close to the viewfinder. Scan the surroundings beforehand for any unwanted features, and leave a generous margin as safety. It is a good idea to negotiate with fellow enthusiasts about their final disposition of elbows, etc. Pick out guiding marks through your viewfinder and tell yourself not to swing past them. Straps are another hazard; they have a habit of poking into the shot. One way to deal with this is to use limp straps of a conspicuous colour; the colour will remind you to check, and the limp straps can be tucked into the palm, clear of the trigger finger. If a fluorescent anorak appears on the scene you can stick a few weeds (common, not rare) between you and the offending object, and crouch. Last minute arrivals are a problem, as the bellowed entreaties to get out of the way are picked up by sound video cameras and tape recorders. Nothing must distract from the principal actor on the stage – the train.

It is important to fill the frame. If the view is noted for some feature such as a gas-holder, a castle or a particular hill, then it should form the secondary focal point of interest and complement the locomotive. If the line passes through a pleasant though ordinary landscape, choose trees and buildings that will frame the centre of interest, and not be cropped off at ridiculous points. If the landscape is flat and featureless, then either the sky must have some interesting clouds or steam exhaust, or the engine must fill the frame itself. Remember to let the locomotive come in towards you just that little bit more, as you have to account for that extra width at the edges.

It is tempting to start photographing the train when it is too distant, especially if you are afraid that the locomotive, in the case of steam, will shut off for a slack before it reaches you. Perhaps a short telephoto lens would be better for you. Another solution is to choose a view that has alternatives: raised up to show the steam, or dropped down to let the engine fill the upper part of the frame, while showing something interesting in the lower half or foreground, if the driver should shut off steam.

These points should form a sound basis for obtaining reliably good photographs. Once you have mastered them, you will no doubt want to experiment and produce pictures that catch the eye through their originality.

Right On 22 May 1982 Southern Railway 4-6-0 No 777 *Sir Lamiel* charges through Dent station on the Settle and Carlisle route with the SLOA southbound 'Cumbrian Mountain Pullman'. This picture demonstrates the basic structure of composition found in monochrome photographs: the strong shapes of the bridge arches echo the curves of the boiler front and smoke deflectors, and these contrast with the two white squares and the two triangular trees. All the lines lead the eye to the chimney on the Golden Section, while the red buffer beam shows how the dominant colour jumps out of the page. The head-on viewpoint, minimising any sideways movement, was chosen as Dent is frequently cloudy and dark, which would have needed a wider aperture and/or a slower shutter speed. Fortunately the sun shone, if but weakly, and gave that extra sparkle to a delightful scene.

Camera: Nikon FM with series E36-72mm zoom lens set at 50mm, plus ultraviolet filter. Exposure: 1/250th sec at f4. Film: Kodachrome 64 ASA.

Below On 26 August 1981, again on the Settle and Carlisle line, LNER 'Pacific' No 4498 *Sir Nigel Gresley* emerges from Culgaith Tunnel, north of Appleby, with the southbound 'Cumbrian Mountain Express'. This composition in the primary colours of blue and yellow, and their secondary green, shows how the recessive blue can be dominant if it is bright enough. The Garter blue of *Sir Nigel Gresley* is given an extra boost by the intense colour of the cloudless sky, and the contrasting yellow of the dry grass in the cutting. On a monochrome level the strongest contrasts are found in the white steam and black smoke, and in the silhouette of the black front against the sunny bank, all in the focus-of-interest area. Notice too how the eye is carried to the front of the engine by the slopes of the bank and the shape of the trees on the skyline.

Camera: Nikon FM with 50mm lens plus ultraviolet filter. Exposure: 1/500th sec at f4.5. Film: Kodachrome 64 ASA.

Above left 'Jubilee' Class 4-6-0 No 5690 *Leander* climbs through Chinley on 24 February 1979 with a Guide Bridge-York special, illustrating the use of dynamic diagonals and a triangular structure composition. The location makes use of the last of the winter snow to reflect more light on to the sides of the locomotive in an otherwise dark cutting. The snow also enhances the visual impact of the white steam and the white panels of the carriage.

Camera: Nikon FM with 50mm lens plus ultraviolet filter. Exposure: 1/250th see at f5.6. Film: Kodachrome 64 ASA.

Left Preserved 'Deltic' No 9000 *Royal Scots Grey* nears Kings Sutton on 21 August 1999 with the 12.10 (Saturdays-only) Ramsgate to Birmingham New Street train. Note the subtle range of green tones in the landscape and locomotive, and the red of the carriages, all of which complement each other.

Camera: Nikon FM with 50mm lens plus ultraviolet filter. Exposure: 1/500th sec at f4. Film: Kodachrome 64 ASA.

Above On 10 November 1995 LMS Class 4F 0-6-0 No 4422 is seen at Kinchley Lane on the Great Central Railway hauling an afternoon Loughborough to Leicester North train. The lustrous black of the locomotive is accentuated by the vibrant autumn colours of the trees and grass. *Malcolm Ranieri*

Camera: Mamiya M645 PRO TL with 80mm lens. Exposure: 1/250th sec at f4.5. Film: Fujichrome Velvia rated at 50 ASA.

Above left Posing at Didcot Steam Centre on the evening of 3 October 1998 is GWR 'Castle' Class 4-6-0 No 4079 *Caerphilly Castle*, which had just returned to the UK after a lengthy sojourn in Australia. This 'night shoot' was organised by the GW Society, Didcot Steam Centre being its headquarters. The tungsten-based film used gives naturalistic colour values. *Malcolm Ranieri*

Camera: Mamiya M645 1000S with 80mm lens, tripod-mounted. Exposure: 20 sec at f8. Film: Fujichrome 64T.

Left The evening sun glints on South African Railways Class '14CR' 4-8-2 No 1897 as it shunts at Riversdale on the Worcester-George line. This picture shows another way of making the most of the available light. The setting sun reflects off the rails at one point, so that the photographer knows exactly where the engine will glitter most brightly. Whatever the colour of the locomotive, it will show as orange, the colour of the sun. With this type of 'glint' shot great care must be taken to shield the camera lens from the rays of the sun, otherwise the picture will be spoiled by excessive flare.

Camera: Nikkormat with 50mm lens plus ultraviolet filter. Exposure: 1/250th sec at f4. Film: Kodachrome 64 ASA.

Above LNER Gresley Class 'K4' 2-6-0 No 3442 heads a Fort William to Mallaig train near Fassfern on the morning of 24 July 1989. Obviously you have to choose your location carefully to obtain a reflection shot, but at the end of the day a certain amount of good luck is needed for a successful picture – sunshine and a lack of wind, as well as, of course, the tide being in.

Camera: Nikon FM with 50mm lens plus ultraviolet filter. Exposure: 1/500th sec at f4. Film: Kodachrome 64 ASA.

Opposite above Being serviced at Povoa shed, northern Portugal, on the evening of 24 September 1974 is No E142, one of four narrow-gauge 2-8-2T engines built by Henschel in 1931. When the engine and its surroundings are black, there is not much point in taking a colour picture unless you can find something colourful to relieve the gloom. This picture shows two possibilities – the background and the workers. The buildings at the back, with their red roofs and immaculate white walls, throw the black engine into strong relief, while the workmen are wearing blue and orange shirts, forming a secondary focus of interest.

Camera: Nikkormat with 50mm lens plus ultraviolet filter. Exposure: 1/125th sec at f5.6. Film: Agfa CT18 rated at 50 ASA.

Left On 24 March 1972 at Cadley Hill Colliery near Burton upon Trent, Hunslet 0-6-0ST *Cadley Hill No 1* takes a load of empty wagons from the exchange sidings to the colliery. The old hawthorn tree provides a perfect frame for this smart-looking engine, and the whole scene is illuminated by crisp spring sunshine.

Camera: Nikkormat with 50mm lens plus ultraviolet filter. Exposure: 1/500th sec at f4. Film: Kodachrome 64 ASA.

Above left This picture was taken inside the cab of a South African Railways Class 24 2-8-4 locomotive at George on 26 July 1976. It would have been almost impossible to have taken this picture without using a medium wide angle lens. As it was, I stood right at the back of the cab in order to get a reasonable coverage of this beautiful footplate. The lighting was even and diffuse, coming from three sides of the cab, which showed the polished copper and brass to good advantage. If the sun had been shining directly on the fittings, the intense highlights and shadows would have lost the colour of the metal. The fire had cooled down to a pleasing red; if it had been roaring at full blast it would have only shown up as a yellow square.

Camera: Nikkormat with 35mm lens plus ultraviolet filter. Exposure: 1/60th sec at f2.8. Film: Kodachrome 64 ASA.

Above right Sunset at Capital Park shed, Pretoria. The date is 13 August 1982 and the locomotive is Class 15 CA 4-8-2 No 2852. This dramatic mood picture relies for its impact on the brilliant red of the sunset. To obtain direct shots of the disc of the sun, it is advisable to wait until the last moment before the sun finally sets, when the haze in the atmosphere filters the light to a usable level, so avoiding the risk of flare. Also, to make the sun appear larger in proportion to the scene, a medium telephoto lens was used.

Camera: Nikon FM with 135mm lens plus ultraviolet filter. Exposure: 1/125th sec at f5.6. Film: Kodachrome 25 ASA.

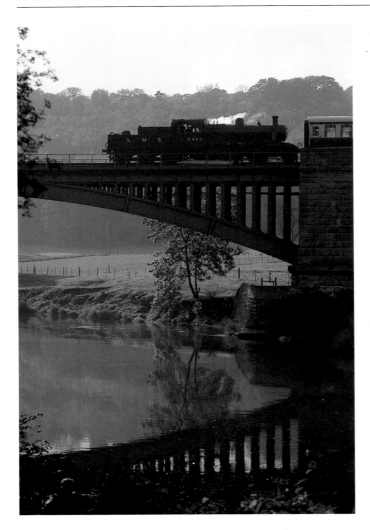

Left This beautiful setting is Victoria Bridge on the Severn Valley Railway, and the scene shows LMS 'Mogul' No 6443 with a Bridgnorth-Bewdley train on 14 October 1979. This peaceful river scene is composed almost entirely of shades of green. Like the previous picture of the sunset, it has strong monochrome construction, with the greatest tonal contrast appearing at the focus of interest. Trees play an important part here – the central tree leads the eye to the engine, while the fringe of branches at the left-hand edge helps to 'anchor' the free end of the bridge.

Camera: Nikon FM with 85mm lens plus ultraviolet filter. Exposure: 1/500th sec at f5.6. Film: Kodachrome 64 ASA.

Below 'Deltic' No 55007 *Pinza* bursts under Holgate Junction bridge and into the evening sunshine as it leaves York with the 19.10 train to King's Cross on 24 May 1981. One way to photograph a long thin shape is to accentuate the form by enclosing it in a narrow slot – here the massive structure of the bridge and its shadow trap the 'Deltic' like the teeth of a crocodile. This approach is the reverse of the upper picture, where the engine is dark against a lighter background; here the train appears bright and colourful contrasted against the black girders.

Camera: Nikon FM with 50mm lens plus ultraviolet filter. Exposure: 1/250th sec at f5.6. Film: Kodachrome 64 ASA.

4
Railway photography – general principles

What makes a good railway photograph? Is it the location, the lighting, the time of year? All these and many more ingredients will help to produce a picture that has atmosphere and interest, and one that will hold the viewer's attention. All these aspects will be discussed in later chapters. But here I want to deal specifically with the basis of general railway photography, that is the photographic approach to the different types of traction (large or small). I have divided them into four categories: steam, diesel, electric, and miniature.

To obtain interesting photographs of any type of traction, certain problems and peculiarities present themselves to the photographer, and once you know how to approach and overcome them you should then have a good basis from which to produce interesting pictures. Once this basic standard has been achieved it opens the door to far more creative aspects, which will also be discussed in detail later on.

Steam

The magic of steam! A great many people would assume that you have only to point the camera at a steam engine, press the shutter release and 'hey presto', a master shot. This is not the case – far from it. Many people would agree that in most cases the very essence of a good steam action picture is for the locomotive to be throwing out smoke and steam; thus the first basic rule is, if at all possible, to take your picture from a location where you know that the engine will be working hard, as for example on a steep incline, or leaving a station or speed-restricted section. Having said that, remember that there are occasions when the locations and lighting conditions are so photogenic that they can compensate for the lack of exhaust from the locomotive.

As steam engines come in all shapes and sizes it follows that certain photographic angles suit certain engines. Some engines may photograph better from a low angle, looking up at them, while other types may be more photogenic from above. And of course the photographer will have his own particular favourite angles for different engines. For example, I like to photograph 'A4' 'Pacifics' from a low

viewpoint because I feel that they have a very powerful streamlined front end, which, when photographed from this angle (especially with a good exhaust), gives a feeling of power and speed, both of which are essentials of any good action photograph. The opposite I feel is true when photographing *King George V*. Here the graceful lines of Great Western engines are shown to best advantage when taken from above.

It does not always work out like this. There are many times when the location itself dictates the angle from which you photograph the locomotive. For example, when photographing around the Diggle and Standedge area (on the Manchester-Huddersfield-Leeds route), which abounds in beautiful, wild photogenic scenery, the landscape cries out to be included in your picture; thus, regardless of the type of locomotive, the best approach is to photograph from above. Remember, though, that in some hill or mountain locations, if the line is above the valley floor crossing a river, for example, a camera level at or below line level may make the scene more dramatic or might be necessary in order to get a natural hill or mountain-top skyline within the camera frame. But in general, when in ordinary surroundings where there is little if any outstanding scenery (and in practice, many locations are like this), the locomotive becomes the dominant part of the composition. In these situations it is worth experimenting with photographic angles to achieve as photogenic a picture as is possible.

Another very important point to remember, and this applies when photographing any type of traction, is that when you are taking action photographs it is important to use a shutter speed fast enough to freeze the train in action. If your shutter speed is too slow, it usually results in movement or blur on the front end of the locomotive, making an unsatisfactory picture. For example, if it is a bright day with plenty of light and you have a medium-speed film in your camera of, say, around 125 ASA, and assuming that you are using a standard lens on your camera, you should have a meter reading giving a shutter speed of 1/500th sec with a lens aperture of around f5.6 to f8 This shutter speed should enable you to freeze most trains in action and to get a reasonably wide angle on the

subject. In the case of HSTs, electrics and fast diesel trains it would be advisable to increase the shutter speed to 1/1000th sec and open the lens aperture to f4 or f5.6, or alternatively stay on the previous camera setting (1/500th at f5.6 to f8) and narrow the angle to freeze the movement of the train. On the other hand, if it is a dull day (as is so often the case!) with a meter reading of 1/250th sec at f2.8 to f4, you need to narrow the angle to slow the relative movement of the train in order to stop the action. In other words, the faster the train and/or the wider the angle from which you take your photograph, the higher the shutter speed required. The slower the train and/or the narrower the angle of the picture, the slower the shutter speed that can be used and still freeze the action.

Another point to bear in mind when taking action photographs is that the greater the distance that the camera is away from the train, the less the movement, which enables you to use a slower shutter speed and smaller lens aperture (giving greater focal length). The nearer you are to the train the relatively greater is the movement, which means that you need a faster shutter speed to freeze the action. At the same time, by increasing your shutter speed you must open up the lens to a wider aperture (which decreases the focal length).

In circumstances where it is really dull and you are down to 1/125th sec at f2.8, it might be worthwhile trying either a panned shot (see Chapter 5) or (mainly in the case of steam locomotives) what is known as a three-quarter rear shot. This simply means photographing the locomotive as it is going away from you, when the movement can be stopped with a slower shutter speed because, with the locomotive at the far end of the train, its relative movement is reduced. It is worthwhile trying this type of shot not only in dull lighting conditions, but also in normal circumstances. Many interesting railway photographs have been taken from this angle, and it could be a mistake to regard it as a second shot to be taken as an extra after the normal first shot, which is usually a three-quarter front

Steam hard at work in a classical setting is well portrayed in this shot of 'Jubilee' Class 4-6-0 No 5690 *Leander* climbing near Ais Gill summit with the southbound SLOA 'Cumbrian Mountain Express'. The precise location is Ais Gill viaduct and the date is 28 January 1982. The dull conditions, which meant using a fairly wide aperture, warranted the use of a medium wide angle lens with its greater depth of field, while at the same time no distortion is discernible. It will also be noted that, as the train was not travelling fast, a 1/250th sec shutter speed was sufficient to freeze the action.

Camera: Nikon FM with 35mm medium wide angle lens plus yellow filter. Exposure: 1/250th sec at f3.5. Film: Ilford XP1 rated at 400 ASA, developed in XP1 chemicals.

view of the train. If you want a really good 'going-away shot' it is far better to concentrate on that alone, and achieve what you require rather than taking a snatched shot hoping that it will turn out to be a good one (that is unless you are using a motor drive that should give you a chance of good shots both ways).

A final word of caution on the use of shutter speeds in action photography: try to avoid using shutter speeds of less than 1/250th sec (with the exception of panned and 'going-away shots') because it is doubtful if a 1/125th or certainly 1/60th sec would stop a train, even almost head-on, and at the same time, when using speeds as slow as 1/60th, you may start to encounter camera shake.

Another problem that arises from time to time when photographing steam locomotives is when they are running in reverse, with the tender or bunker (in the case of tank engines) nearer the camera. Unlike locomotives facing forward (smokebox first), it is pointless to photograph them head-on or from too narrow an angle, otherwise all you will get in your picture is a photograph of a tender or bunker. In these circumstances you need to take as wide an angle as possible (shutter speed permitting) and from a reasonable distance in order to get a good side view of the engine and train in a landscape setting, which in turn should make for a more interesting picture.

Diesel

It would be fair to say that on the whole the diesel locomotive is not as obviously photogenic as its steam counterpart, and this in itself most certainly provides a challenge to the photographer of modern traction.

Unlike steam, where a good exhaust alone can make an atmospheric picture, when photographing diesel traction you need to make as much use of lighting and location as possible in order to create atmosphere. And that is where you have a decided advantage in Britain, for unlike steam trains, which only run on certain days on certain specific BR routes and preserved lines, diesel trains are running seven days a week the length and breadth of the country, although the incidence of locomotive-hauled passenger trains is steadily dwindling. In consequence you are more or less able to choose the sort of lighting and locations that should lead to good atmospheric pictures. This is well borne out by the many fine photographs to be seen today in modern traction books and magazines.

As with steam locomotives, some types of diesels look better than others from certain angles. I always felt that a 'Deltic' was more photogenic when photographed from a low angle, accentuating the aggressive-looking front end and giving a genuine impression of a powerful locomotive

at work. But again, the photographer will have his or her own favourite angles for different types of locomotive, and with any type of traction it is well worth experimenting to find the most photogenic angles.

The lack of exhaust in diesels (at least in the best maintained examples) can be made up to a certain extent by the use of a good sky effect. Unlike steam, you can pick your day and moment when photographing modern traction. Wait until you have a good sunny day with plenty of white fluffy clouds, fit a yellow or red filter to your camera lens (if taking black and white) and go out and try your hand. You will be surprised at the effect and impact a good cloud effect can have on your composition, adding life and atmosphere (see page 18).

Another good effect with which to create atmosphere in a modern traction picture is to photograph the train as it tilts away from you on a curve. This gives an impression of imbalance and, thus, movement. Experiment with lighting conditions, especially early morning and evening when you have low sunlight. Tremendous lighting effects (which of course can add great impact to your pictures) can be created, especially when taking your photographs with extreme back lighting (*contre-jour*), thus getting a golden glow on the side of the train. These are commonly known as 'glint shots' (see Chapter 6 for further technical details). Splendid effects can also be obtained in winter, especially when there is a sprinkling of snow around, but more about that in a later chapter.

Another effective way to photograph modern traction (or any type of traction for that matter) is the reflection shot. This simply means that you mirror the locomotive or train in water so that your picture consists of the actual locomotive and train together with its reflected image. If you are taking station or shed shots the reflection could be in a pool of water created by a sudden shower, or if you are out in the country or near the coast good reflections are possible when the train is crossing over a river, stream or

On 6 June 1981 a southbound DMU crosses the High Level bridge at Newcastle with an evening local train. The evening light accentuates the structures of the bridge as well as the train and the surrounding features, which makes for a harmonious composition. This type of setting is very photogenic for any type of traction, but even more so when photographing modern traction, the lighting and location, together with the repeating bridge patterns, providing the dramatic interest. This train could have been photographed a few feet further on, but by shooting at this position the arch of the bridge leads the eye to the front of the train.

Camera: Nikon FM with 85mm lens plus yellow filter. Exposure: 1/250th sec at f5.6. Film: Ilford FP4 rated at 160 ASA, developed in Aculux.

estuary. But the water must be fairly calm, otherwise you will not get a good reflection, so obviously avoid wet and windy days for this type of picture.

Make as much use of locations as is possible. There are many fine viaducts, bridges, stations, and even some surviving signal boxes and semaphore signals to incorporate into your picture. Remember when photographing modern traction you can more or less choose the weather and to a great extent the location – but always avoid trespassing.

Electric

Most of the points mentioned in the diesel section apply almost equally well when photographing electric traction, especially on the third-rail system. But with overhead catenary, certain obvious problems present themselves and you should be fairly selective when photographing this type of electric traction from above, although there is plenty of scope for good electric traction photographs taken from the side and three-quarter front and rear. This is especially so when they are photographed from a reasonable distance and therefore incorporated into the landscape. For example, make use of trees to frame the picture, or maybe a river or flooded field in order to create a strong foreground. The catenary masts themselves, with their receding pattern, also provide a strong visual feature that can be made to enhance a photograph. All these and many more elements will help to make far more interesting photographs of what is not an easy subject to tackle. Certainly photographing overhead electric traction is a challenge to the railway photographer, but one that can be overcome with a certain amount of thought and, of course, experiment.

Miniature railways

Miniature railways – and by miniature I mean railways of 15-inch gauge or less – are often neglected in railway photography, much to its detriment, I feel. In Britain alone there are many splendid lines of various gauges spread throughout the country, which feature many fine examples of British and overseas locomotives, mostly working steam models as well as many freelance designs. Many of the railways are situated in highly photogenic locations such as parks or woodland, and some have fine railway buildings, signals, bridges, etc, all of which can contribute to better railway photography. Some of the 15-inch-gauge lines, such as the Romney, Hythe & Dymchurch in South East England and the Ravenglass & Eskdale in the Lake District, were built as a means of transport for the local population, as opposed to the tourist lines that they are today.

This picture is an example of how you can use natural surroundings to frame the locomotive and, by taking from a side view, use the frame (in this case trees) to cut out the catenary masts, etc. It is important that when taking trains from this angle, especially as in this case with the train travelling at high speed, to use a very fast shutter. A 135mm lens (in 35mm size) was deliberately used in this instance to keep the foreground blurred and the train reasonably sharp, focusing the attention on the subject. The location is Norton Bridge Junction, north of Stafford, and the train is a northbound Inter-City hauled by Class 86 No 86231 on 15 April 1982.

Camera, Nikon FM with 135mm lens. Exposure 1/1000th sec at f6.3. Film, Ilford XP1 (400 ASA), developed in XP1 chemicals.

This is the standard three-quarter front shot as applied to overhead electric traction. The tilt of the locomotive on the cant of the curve helps to provide an impression of movement, and the framing of the train with the catenary provides a more balanced picture. The location is Milford, south of Stafford, and the train is a southbound freight hauled by Class 86 locomotive No 86032 on 15 April 1982.

Camera: Nikon FM with 85mm lens plus yellow filter. Exposure: 1/1000th sec at f6.3. Film: Ilford XP1, developed in XP1 chemicals.

This picture and the one overleaf illustrate the two distinct approaches to miniature railway photography. The first photograph, of *River Esk* of the Ravenglass & Eskdale Railway on the turntable at Ravenglass station on 21 August 1975, shows the true scale of the miniature locomotive by the deliberate inclusion of people.

Camera: Nikkormat with 50mm lens plus yellow filter. Exposure: 1/500th sec at f8. Film: Ilford FP4 rated at 200 ASA, developed in Acuspecial.

There are two major ways in which to approach miniature railway photography. Because of the size of the locomotives and trains you can deliberately include people such as the driver and passengers (especially children) in your picture and make them part of the railway scene, thus giving your photographs the true scale of miniature railways. This is probably much the best way to photograph the smallest gauges. But it is also possible to approach 15-inch-gauge railways from the other angle; that is, to try and make the locomotives and trains appear as if they were full size.

Obviously this second approach is far from easy, but by careful and thoughtful photography it is possible on occasions to make the little ones look like their big brothers on the main line. One way is to photograph the train almost head-on as it pulls out of a station; if the exhaust is strong enough it should obscure the driver and any passengers. But make sure that the background is something like trees or bushes so that the size of the train is not given away as it would be if, for example, you took it against a background of houses.

The other method that can be used, but which requires some patience on the part of the photographer, is to wait until a train has discharged its passengers at a terminus station and the driver has gone off for a quick break, then, without people around to give away the scale of the locomotive and train, together with a bit of ingenuity and luck, it is possible to obtain a more 'main-line' type of picture.

One very important point to remember is that because of their obviously smaller size, you will have to be that much nearer to get a balanced picture, in which case you will need to use a small aperture (high f number) in order to get a good depth of field. If you are photographing a locomotive from, say, 6 feet and you use too large an aperture (low f number) you will find the front of the locomotive sharp, but the back end out of focus, with any coaches behind as a blur.

But however you approach the photography of miniature railways, you will be amazed by the sheer beauty of the locomotives and their likeness to their big brothers, by the care and attention given them by their enthusiastic owners and, last but not least, by the enjoyment they bring to many thousands of people, young and old alike. It all helps to make photographing these little beauties so rewarding and such a pleasure.

The Romney, Hythe & Dymchurch locomotive No 10 *Dr Syn* pulls out of Hythe on 30 March 1975. This scene is a deliberate attempt to convey the opposite impression from the previous photograph. By getting more of the front-end view and adopting a fairly low angle, coupled with an exhaust that hides the driver, the impression is almost one of the main line. But for shots like this you do need luck, especially as in this case with the exhaust.

Camera: Nikkormat with 85mm lens plus yellow filter.
Exposure: 1/500th sec at f8. Film: Ilford FP4, rated at 200 ASA, developed in Acuspecial.

5
Style, composition and techniques

Style

With all art forms (and I certainly regard photography as an art form) there is usually more than one approach or style, and railway photography is certainly no exception. Being also a musician with a love of jazz, I find that railway photography, like jazz, can be divided into three distinct approaches: traditional, mainstream and modern.

The style of the traditional approach can be described simply as the classic three-quarter front view of the locomotive and train in action with the accent on the train rather than the scenery and surroundings. This style was very much the hallmark of such early railway photographers as the Rev T. B. Parley and Dr T. F. Budden, and perfected by F. E. Mackay and H. Gordon Tidey. A glance through *The Railway Magazine* of the period between 1910 and the late 1920s will show many fine examples of this approach. But as I mentioned in the Introduction, photographers of this period were very much limited by their heavy and cumbersome equipment and it was only at the end of the 1920s and early 1930s that styles began to change.

There were a number of reasons for this, but principal among them was the advent of smaller and very much lighter cameras using roll film instead of plates. A new style thus emerged, which I have called the mainstream approach. This used the best of the older traditional style, that is good sharp pictures of trains in action, still usually with a three-quarter front viewpoint, but now employed a very much more pictorial approach to the subject, incorporating in the picture far more of the railway and surrounding scenery.

Since its inception the pictorial approach has remained with us as a leading style in railway photography. And why not? It incorporates both old and new and for a lot of people would seem to convey the very essence and atmosphere of the railway scene. But we must not turn our backs on anything new. Certainly the modern or New Approach (as it became popularly known) to railway photography, pioneered by Colin Gifford, John Hunt, Ian Krause and others in the 1960s, added an exciting and very realistic dimension to the medium.

With this approach the accent was on the whole railway scene, and in many instances the train was of lesser

This picture of Class 'A2' 'Pacific' No 60532 *Blue Peter* near Plean Junction on 18 June 1966 with an Aberdeen-Glasgow express is a traditional three-quarter front style of photograph. The train dominates the scene, but the features of the locomotive and the exhaust make up for the lack of scenery.

Camera: Konica range-finder with 45mm lens plus yellow filter. Exposure: 1/500th sec at f4. Film: Kodak Plus X rated at 125 ASA, developed in D76 (undiluted).

significance in relation to the scene depicted in the photograph. A good example would be a picture of a freight train passing through its natural industrial environment, a scene full of factories, chimneys and smoke; by putting the accent on the industrial scene as a whole and not just the train, the impression of a freight in its natural settings is conveyed.

Another example of the modern style is to photograph men at work. It could be a booking clerk, shunter, driver, signalman or any of a host of other people who work on the railways. Passengers, too, can make very interesting studies, and the New Approach was certainly a pioneer in the human involvement in the railway scene. But a word of warning: to capture this type of picture you have sometimes only a few seconds in which to work. A delay and the magic moment may be past. It is never quite the same if people pose for photographs – there is nearly always an air of self-consciousness about 'posed' pictures.

This modern approach certainly seems to fit in well when photographing modern traction, giving added impetus to what in some cases could be a rather flat subject. Generally this type of photography calls for more creative thought on the part of the cameraman, which in many cases should produce pictures of an imaginative and creative nature. Very often photographs are taken with what can be called 'available light', that is minimum or poor natural light, which with fast films can achieve presentable results even inside buildings without flash – a gloomy interior of an engine shed can be captured as it really is.

To conclude this section on the different approaches to railway photography, the three main styles can be summarised thus:

Traditional

This style of railway photography is basically a three-quarter front view of the locomotive and train, mainly to the exclusion of the surroundings, etc, but very useful to give an impact picture of a train hard at work – particularly steam – and of course when the surroundings do not warrant too much inclusion in the picture. It requires good photographic technique (as indeed do all styles) to execute properly.

Mainstream

This middle-of-the-road or pictorial approach has much to offer and allows the photographer plenty of scope in his or her compositions. It certainly seems to be a very useful style for depicting the steam scene.

Modern

This New Approach allows the photographer freedom of expression and creativity, and is arguably very suitable when applied to modern traction.

All of these styles have much to offer railway photographers and should form a firm base on which you can then build your own individual ideas, and possibly one day help to create a style of your own.

Composition

By composition we mean the lines that draw the eye to the focus of interest, and give a feeling of balance to the picture. We often choose a location for a photograph with an intuitive sense of composition, which is in fact developed over years of looking at famous works of art and good quality photographs in advertising. Often we perceive a master shot without being aware of the mechanics of the composition, and select the stance and lens to achieve it. Sometimes, of course, the situation is far from ideal; other photographers may have got there first and courtesy demands that the latecomer does not obstruct their view. Sometimes the train comes early and catches the photographer unprepared, but the resulting snatched shot can sometimes be turned into an exciting composition by means of careful cropping.

We should study the paintings of the great masters of the Renaissance and after, for it was in this period that artists came to grips with the problems of perspective and foreshortening, using a viewing device known as the 'camera obscura'. This was a box with a lens at the front and a mirror within, which transmitted the landscape on to a baseboard, albeit very dimly, where the artist could mark out the scene. Every artist had his recognisable style, as indeed have great photographers, but all depended on a limited number of constructions that were acceptable to the public. Rubens is famous for his curves – or perhaps for his curvaceous forms. The Dutch painter Hobbema is famous for his view down a straight road lined with tall trees, an ideal example of the use of perspective. In this section I shall demonstrate some of these popular constructions, and illustrate them with photographs.

It was the French painter Ingres who held the opinion that 'Drawing includes everything except the tint'. Although this takes little account of the emotional impact of the use of colour, dealt with in the section on colour photography, it underlines the importance of good composition. No picture will be satisfying unless it fulfils certain requirements, relying on either linear structure or repeated rhythms of shape and pattern, or, as generally happens, a combination of several aspects.

The Golden Section

The principal rule of composition is the so-called 'Golden Section', which was discovered by the Ancient Greeks and was a proportional ratio used throughout the temple buildings of the Acropolis. The relationship of the parts is expressed by the formula $\frac{a}{b} = \frac{b}{(a+b)}$, or approximately 1:1.6, as can be seen in Figure 5. In practice this means that the most interesting place for your locomotive is just off centre in the photograph. By following the rule of the Golden Section there is a choice of four positions, as indicated by the extra dotted lines. In most conventional railway photography, the point chosen would be one of the two lower positions, because the photographer often stands up on a bank or bridge and looks down on the train. But if you were looking upwards, one of the upper positions would probably be your choice. It should be noted that when photographing steam engines, the focus of interest falls behind the smokebox door and underneath the chimney, not on the buffer beam, as the directional lines often run through the exhaust, leading the eye to that part of the engine. If the photographer takes liberties with this proportion, there must be a good reason, and the dramatic tension must be balanced by some compensating factor, such as a very powerful exhaust, or significant detail in the foreground.

Other principles of composition are demonstrated by the following photographs and diagrams.

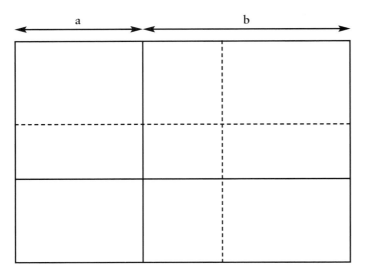

Figure 5: The rectangle divided by the Golden Sections into four possible focal points of interest.

Triangle

Right This is often found on railways because the parallel lines of the rails and rolling-stock, following the rules of perspective, slope towards the vanishing point in the distance. This is very clear here, with the upper side of the triangle following an invisible line through the tilt of the driver's cap. This tiny detail, perceived unconsciously, is so important to the composition and guides the photographer's finger to press the shutter *now* and not 2 seconds later. Notice that the secondary focus of interest, where the driver emerges from the cab, falls on the top right Golden Section. The photograph was taken on the Fairbourne Railway near Barmouth (15-inch gauge) on 8 August 1973, as trains hauled by *Katie* and *Sian* are about to pass each other at the crossing loop.

Camera: Nikkormat with 50mm lens plus yellow filter. Exposure: 1/250th sec at f8. Film: Ilford FP4 rated at 200 ASA, developed in Acuspecial.

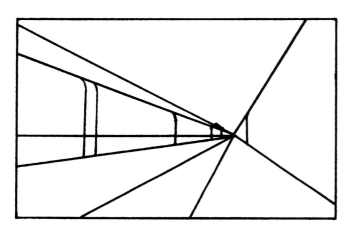

Starburst

Left On the morning of 31 October 1981 a pair of Class 25s, Nos 25062 and 25027, wait to leave Bewdley on the Severn Valley Railway with the SVR 'Cathedrals Express' to Paddington via Worcester and Oxford. The lines of perspective lead to a vanishing point, a structure that is frequently met in the railway scene, when a train is either approaching or departing. This static scene is given dramatic interest by placing the mysteriously hidden destination well to the right of centre. The low viewpoint helps to make the right-hand roofline slope more steeply, a trick that stimulates a feeling of movement. Notice the reflections in the high gloss of the carriage on the right, without which the shadows would be much too heavy, and also how the wiggly rail reflections are repeated in the cable on the ground.

Camera: Zeiss Super Ikonta 531-16 6x6cm folding camera with 75mm lens. Exposure: 1/100th sec at f5.6. Film: Ilford FP4 rated at 125 ASA, developed in ID11 (undiluted).

Triangle

At Povoa in northern Portugal on 20 September 1974, metre-gauge 2-6-0 tank No 103 gets the final once over before leaving with the 12.32 to Porto. In this picture the triangle lies on the chimney (apex) and buffer beam (base), but the points of the triangle are completed by the two railway staff, particularly by the one with the bent leg – another critical moment for shutter release. Notice that the object of the inspector's interest falls on the Golden Section. This picture is also enhanced by the repeating rhythm of circles.

Camera: Nikkormat with 50mm lens plus yellow filter. Exposure: 1/500th sec at f5.6.
Film: Ilford FP4 rated at 200 ASA, developed in Acuspecial.

Dynamic Diagonals

Sloping lines tend to create a feeling of movement. Here the camber of the bend naturally tilts Vale of Rheidol Railway 2-6-2 tank No *9 Prince of Wales* as it approaches Devil's Bridge station on 9 August 1973 with a train from Aberystwyth, and gives it extra punch as it snorts out of the cutting. It follows that a good place to catch an engine at speed is head-on coming round a bend (which position helps to freeze the movement if the photographer cannot use a fast shutter speed). Some stations are built on a curving track that is banked for non-stop trains, and a static shot by a platform can be given extra life by catching the engine in a tilted position.

Camera: Nikkormat with 50mm lens plus yellow filter. Exposure: 1/250th sec at f2.8. Film: Ilford FP4 rated at 200 ASA, developed in Acuspecial.

Dynamic diagonals

The slanted viewpoint of this crew change at York on 23 May 1981 has turned all parallels and right angles into diagonals. Notice how the slope of the cage holding the mailbags carries the eye to the pointing finger.

Camera: Nikon FM with 50mm lens. Exposures: 1/125th sec at f4. Film: Ilford FP4 rated at 160 ASA, developed in Aculux.

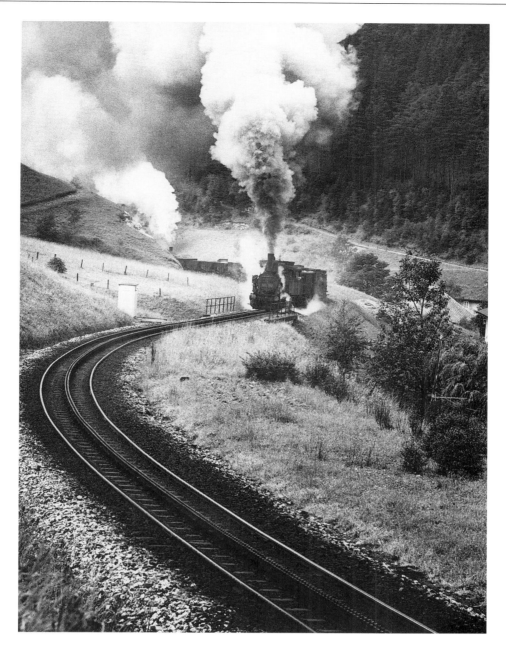

Hogarth Spiral, or vertical spiral

The painter Hogarth developed this device for composing society portraits of ladies in crinolines and wide-brimmed hats, and in railway photography this device lends itself very naturally to views down reverse curves, finished off with trees or billowing exhausts. This photograph was taken on the famous Vordenberg incline in Southern Austria on 28 August 1974, with a pair of 97 Class rack locomotives (Nos 97-209 and 97-201) en route to Markt with iron ore empties.

Camera: Nikkormat with 85mm lens plus yellow filter. Exposure: 1/250th sec at f8.
Film: Ilford FP4 rated at 160 ASA, developed in Acutol.

Flat spiral

DB 012 'Pacific' No 012 055 near Meppen, Germany, with an Emden-Rheine express on 21 March 1975. This location was chosen to display the plume of smoke to the greatest advantage. The spirals in the top half run in opposite directions to those in the lower half, creating extra interest. If the wind had been blowing from the other side, the curves would have interlocked, forming a whirlpool effect. Notice the importance of the shadow in the foreground, bringing the eye into the subject, and how the clump of trees helps to carry the line of the rails round the corner.

Camera: Nikkormat with 85mm lens plus yellow filter.
Exposure: 1/1000th sec at f5.6. Film: Ilford FP4 rated at 200 ASA, developed in Acuspecial.

Layered effect

Class 'A4' 'Pacific' No 4498 *Sir Nigel Gresley*, on the southbound 'Cumbrian Mountain Express', meets Class 40 No 40194 on a northbound goods. The location is just north of Culgaith on the Settle & Carlisle line on 15 July 1981, a setting chosen for the repeating rhythms of the trees, with the railway line occupying the Golden Section at the bottom. Layered lines can often be found in places like estuaries or in cloud formations. In this instance the 'A4' happily met the Class 40 in the chosen spot, and the shape of this fortunate encounter was echoed in the break in the line of trees in the middle distance.

Camera: Nikon FM with 85mm lens plus yellow filter.
Exposure: 1/500th sec at f5.6. Film: Ilford FP4 rated at
160 ASA, developed in Aculux.

Contrast

LMS 'Jubilee' 4-6-0 *Leander* pulls out of Bridgnorth on the Severn Valley Railway for Hampton Loade on 21 November 1981. In this instance the layered effect is elaborated by a vertical grid of poplar trees. This is a useful device on two counts. First, on a grey day with little variation in the middle tones, the photographer needs as much contrast as possible, supplied here by the dark tree trunks against the light sky. Second, whenever an object is veiled it becomes more intriguing, and the movement of the train behind the boles is a trick to catch the attention. There is also a triangular structure running upwards through the steam and downwards into the weeping willow.

This picture also serves as a good example of what you can achieve in poor lighting conditions. Because there was insufficient light to get a satisfactory three-quarter front position (it would have meant an exposure of 1/250th sec at around f2, which might have frozen the action but there would have been very little depth of field), I decided to try for a 'going-away' shot, in which case the shutter speed of 1/125th sec was sufficient to freeze the action, and the aperture of f3 gave a better depth of field, resulting in a pleasant composition.

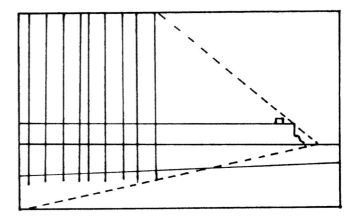

Camera: Nikon FM with 50mm lens. Exposure: 1/125th sec at f3. Film: Ilford XP1 rated at 400 ASA, developed in XP1 chemicals.

Contrast

A northbound HST pulls out of Newcastle Central on 6 June 1981 over the famous diamond crossing, photographed from the castle battlements. Visually the IC125 units do not change and demand resourcefulness on the part of the cameraman to find an original treatment. Here the contrast is provided by the sparkling texture of the crossing lines behind the smooth streamlining of the HST. The picture also contains the elements of the Golden Section, the rhythm of the canopies echoing the curve of the cab, and guiding lines from such features as the retaining wall and the island platforms. Note the detail in the shadow area, which has been retained by holding back during the printing stage.

Camera: Nikon FM 85mm lens plus yellow filter.
Exposure: 1/250th sec at f6.3. Film: Ilford FP4 rated at 160 ASA, developed in Aculux.

Square and circle

That most photogenic of stations, King's Cross, once host to 'A4s', is here the setting for a brace of 'Deltics', now themselves also but a memory, Nos D55019 *Tulyar* and D55009 *Alycidon*, on 20 June 1981. The squareness of the yellow fronts makes a geometric contrast with the circular span of the canopy. This type of composition lends itself well to head-on views of steam engines with side tanks or smoke deflectors, or diesels coming under bridges. A little asymmetry brings the right-hand 'Deltic' on to the Golden Section. These locomotives illustrate the previous remarks on textured backgrounds for plain shapes, and their cab windows repeat the circular rhythms of the roof girders.

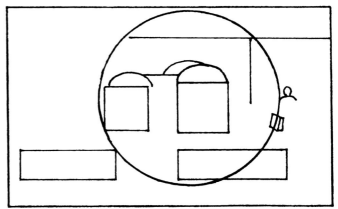

Camera: Nikon FM with 35mm lens. Exposure: 1/60th sec at f4. Film: Ilford Pan F rated at 50 ASA, developed in ID11 (undiluted). Note the beautiful tonal quality of this film.

Repeated shapes

As in some of the previous examples, an outstanding feature is given far more meaning if it is put in a setting of sympathetic shapes. Turkish Railways 2-10-2 No 57016, near Torbali Junction with a Denizli to Izmir train on 23 February 1976, has two domes of interesting outline. Fortunately I spotted a piece of waste ground smoothed by passing feet into mounds of a similar shape, and caught the engine as it was passing it. Shapes can be repeated in reflections, as when an engine crosses a river bridge, or passes a lake.

Camera: Nikkormat with 50mm lens plus yellow filter. Exposure: 1/500th sec at f5.6. Film: Ilford FP4 rated at 160 ASA, developed in Aculux.

Filling the picture

It sometimes happens that the photographer cannot get near enough to the train to fill the frame, and needs something extra to complete the scene. One obvious solution is to use the repeated rhythm, as here where the caravans duplicate the shape of the carriages, and the headland echoes the shape of the smoke of No 4472 *Flying Scotsman* as it climbs near Goodrington with a Paignton-Kingswear train on the Torbay Steam Railway on 21 July 1973. Note the use of a short telephoto lens in this shot, which slightly foreshortens the background and thus emphasises it.

Camera: Nikkormat with 85mm lens plus yellow filter.
Exposure: 1/250th sec at f8. Film: Ilford FP4 rated at 200 ASA,
developed in Acuspecial.

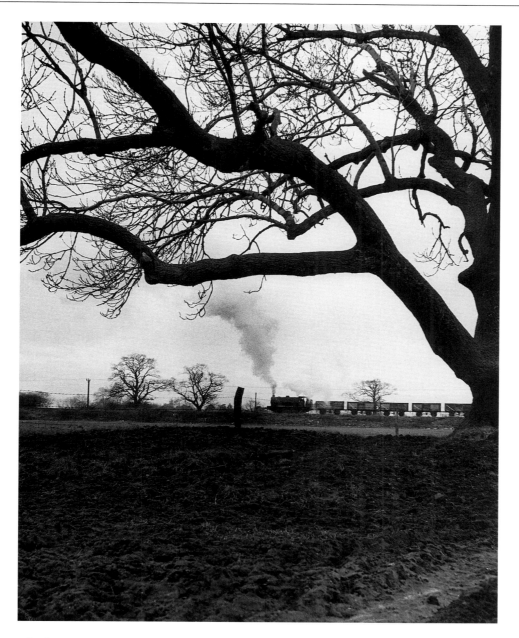

Framing the picture

At Littleton Colliery in Staffordshire, on 2 January 1969, *Littleton No 2*, an 0-6-0 saddle tank, is seen between Penkridge and Boscomoor with empties for the colliery. Not only does the tree fill the sky with an interesting silhouette, but also the direction of its branches is similar to the slant of the exhaust. The tree also reflects the spartan appearance of the industrial railway scene.

Camera: Konica 35mm range-finder with 45mm lens plus yellow filter. Exposure: 1/125th sec at f5.6. Film: Kodak Plus X rated at 125 ASA, developed in D76 (undiluted).

Framing the picture

In a similar way to the previous landscape, where branches were included to fill the top of the composition, here the subject is framed like curtains on a stage. It is fairly easy to find doorways and windows in an engine shed, or in signal boxes, to surround the view of an engine, but by keeping your mind open to the unexpected, and being prepared to climb up or crouch down, you may find some novel ways of achieving this. This buffer stop at the end of a siding makes a window if one is prepared to bend the knees. Notice how the slopes of the buttressing girders help to lead the eye to the train, made up of 0-6-0 saddle tank *Spitfire* and loaded wagons from Bickershaw Colliery near Leigh, Lancashire, heading for the exchange sidings on 21 June 1972.

Camera: Nikkormat with 50mm lens plus yellow filter.
Exposure: 1/125th sec at f11. Film: Kodak Plus X rated at 125 ASA,
developed in D76 (undiluted).

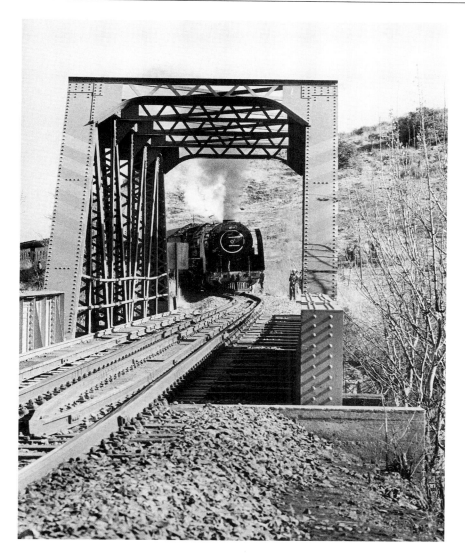

Framing the picture

Many other useful structures are available for framing pictures, such as signals, the yellow cut-out numbers of speed limit signs, brackets, and the latticework of bridges. Sometimes it is a gap between familiar objects that takes on an unexpected shape, such as between the buffers and pipes of carriage couplings. Here South African Railways Class 25 4-8-4 No 3403, photographed near Ficksburg with a Bloemfontein-Bethlehem train on 3 August 1981, is framed in the tunnel of girders, and carries an air of pent-up energy. Notice also how the circle of the boiler is contained in the square of the webbing, and how the engine falls on the Golden Section.

Camera: Nikon FM with 50mm lens plus yellow filter. Exposure: 1/250th see at f8. Film: Ilford FP4 rated at 125 ASA, developed in ID11 (undiluted).

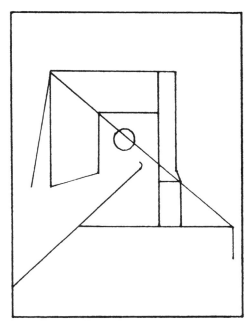

Technique

This section deals with the techniques required for the many different types of pictures that the photographer is able to achieve within the medium of railway photography.

Landscapes

The landscape is probably the most common form of railway photograph, yet in many ways it is one of the most difficult in which to achieve success. The biggest fault of most landscape pictures is trying to get too much of the landscape into the shot, so that the train becomes virtually lost in the panorama. Thus it is important to keep a balance between train and scenery unless there are exceptional features or circumstances that dictate otherwise. A medium telephoto lens can be an asset when you are unable to get near enough to the scene to get the right balance. However, if you use a lens that is too long you get a certain amount of foreshortening, which may distort and spoil the picture.

When you are unable to obtain the right sort of balance in your picture, one idea is to frame the train with an interesting foreground feature such as a tree, gate or fence. This will not only add to the character of the scene but help to spotlight the train.

Below On a murky day at the end of winter, 20 March 1982, LMS 'Pacific' No 6201 *Princess Elizabeth* climbs out of Shrewsbury with a southbound 'Welsh Marches Pullman' at Baystone Hill. This classic pictorial approach of a train in the landscape shows an engine taken at the moment that its buffer beam intersects the line between the fence posts on the left and the base of the tree on the right, so that the chimney falls on the Golden Section. The structure relies on triangles, such as the one formed by the track leading to the bend on the left, then returning up through the meadow on the right to the top of the tree. Another is formed by the same track and bend, but including the height of the exhaust. The beauty of this locomotive is greatly enhanced by the way the oak tree on the right echoes the billowing steam.

Camera: Nikon FM with 50mm lens plus yellow filter. Exposure: 1/500th sec at f4.5. Film: Ilford XP1 rated at 400 ASA, developed in XP1 chemicals.

Right On a sunnier 3 May 1982, the beautiful location is Bull Gill south of Kirkby Stephen on the Settle & Carlisle line, and the train is the southbound 'Cumbrian Mountain Express' hauled by No 34092 *City of Wells*. This picture well illustrates a balanced landscape: strong characteristic foreground interest is combined with a mountainous backdrop (emphasised by the use of a short telephoto lens). Added to this is the strong cloud effect brought about by the use of a yellow filter. The brilliant sunlight enabled me to use a small aperture (with a fast shutter speed), which meant a generous depth of field. Note that everything is in focus, from the house to the hills. Also note that the size of the engine is well in proportion to the overall picture.

Camera: Nikon FM with 85mm lens plus yellow filter. Exposure: 1/500th sec at f9. Film: Ilford XP1 rated 400 ASA, developed in XP1 chemicals.

South African Railways Class 25 4-8-4 No 3515 climbs into Sheridan with the 0745 (Saturdays-only) Bethlehem-Ficksburg train on 24 July 1982, midwinter in the southern hemisphere. In previous years this view had not been attractive because of the clutter of maize stalks, but since the field had been drilled for grass, this seemed an ideal opportunity to use the ribbed surface as a foreground with character. This layered construction enabled me to raise the subject to the upper Golden Section, and its proportions let me take in the whole of the train. The tree behind the guard's van is very important as a counterbalance to the visual weight of the engine, and it forms the other footing for the arch of steam in the sky.

Camera: Nikon FM with 50mm lens plus yellow filter.
Exposure: 1/250th sec at f5.6. Film: Ilford Pan F rated at
50 ASA, developed in ID11 (undiluted).

On the picturesque George-Knysna branch in Cape Province, South African Railways Class 24 2-8-4 No 3652 is caught in silhouette as it crosses the lakes near Rondevlei with the midday branch train. To obtain this shot I filmed from inside the car to shelter the lens from the direct glare of the sun. Whenever there is no detail visible on the engine because it is in silhouette, there should be compensating interest in the surrounding areas. The mudflats on the borders of the lagoon break up the water into a sparkling texture, reflecting the direct morning sunlight. I chose this spot to park the car as the hills rose up into a conspicuous summit at this point, and the only cloud in the sky fitted in very nicely above it. Although the causeway was level, I knew that the engine would be working reasonably hard and the exhaust that I expected would show up clearly against the darker hills.

Camera: Nikon FM with 50mm lens plus yellow filter.
Exposure: 1/500th sec at f8. Film: Ilford FP4 rated at 200 ASA, developed in Acuspecial.

Towns and cities

The industrial landscape of towns and cities obviously differs from the rural landscape just mentioned, but it is just as important to get the right balance between the train and its surroundings, and the same rules apply, although the surroundings are considerably different.

To get the feel of a town or city in your picture it is important to include things that denote its location. For example, a row of neat terraced houses would perhaps give the feeling of a town, while a tower block of flats or offices would represent a city. An industrial scene can easily be created by incorporating cooling towers or large factories in the picture. The possibilities for railway photography in urban and industrial setting are very great and should provide a challenge to the ingenuity of the photographer.

It is worth mentioning here that whether you are photographing in town or the country, home or abroad, if possible always have at hand good detailed maps. This will save time in getting to locations more easily.

The inclusion of the row of neat terraced houses in this picture certainly gives the impression of a train at work in urban surroundings, in this case just west of Stalybridge station; the train is the northbound 'Trans Pennine Pullman' hauled by 'Jubilee' Class 4-6-0 No 5690 *Leander* on 10 April 1982.

Camera: Nikon FM with 85mm lens plus yellow filter.
Exposure: 1/500th sec at f5-6. Film: Ilford XP1 rated at
400 ASA, developed in XP1 chemicals.

By including blocks of flats in this setting for a shot of a Class 47 with a Leeds-York train, we help to create the atmosphere of a city, in this case Leeds. The date is 11 November 1980.

Camera: Nikon FM with 85mm lens plus yellow filter. Exposure: 1/500th sec at f5.6. Film: Ilford FP4 rated at 160 ASA, developed in Aculux.

Cooling towers, factories, pylons and the M6 motorway all combine to produce an industrial setting for this picture of Brush Class 47 No 47341 on an eastbound train of hopper wagons. The location is Bromford Bridge, east of Birmingham, on 14 April 1982.

Camera: Nikon FM with 50mm lens plus yellow filter. Exposure: 1/500th sec at f5.6. Film: Ilford FP4 rated at 200 ASA, developed in Acuspecial.

Bridges and viaducts

Many of us are fascinated by bridges and viaducts. The sight of the Forth Bridge or Ribblehead Viaduct often makes us think of man's tremendous battle against nature and the elements when they were constructed. Many of these magnificent structures are very photogenic in their own right, and if you add the presence of a train you have a complete railway scene full of beauty and interest. But there is an art to photographing such structures, and you cannot approach it without thought and expect to get good results.

As with locomotives, certain types of viaducts and bridges look better from particular angles. With some river bridges, for example, you may decide to film from a low angle, not only because it may be more photogenic, but also simply to include the riverside scene of boats, etc, and, if the water is calm enough, reflections of the train.

However, be careful when filming from lower angles as many bridges and viaducts have quite high parapets that will obscure part of the train. One way to deal with this, if there is a clear section at the end of the bridge or viaduct, is to wait until the locomotive and part of the train has reached this, then photograph it; by so doing you will only obscure the rear part of the train. With viaducts, because they generally span valleys, it may be better to take a view from above, if possible, to include the surrounding hills and slopes in your picture.

These suggestions are meant only as guidelines, and a certain amount of experiment may be necessary before satisfactory results are achieved.

There will be certain physical problems when photographing many viaducts and bridges; the main one is when you are unable to get close enough to the subject to get a reasonably balanced picture. This can be overcome to a certain extent by the use of telephoto lenses; these are ideal for taking scenes side-on, but when filming from the three-quarter front position if you use extra-long telephoto lenses you may find that the viaduct or bridge becomes too distorted by foreshortening.

There are also times when a wide angle lens is very useful, especially when shooting a scene from a lower angle. By using this lens you are able to get close into the subject and still achieve a balanced picture.

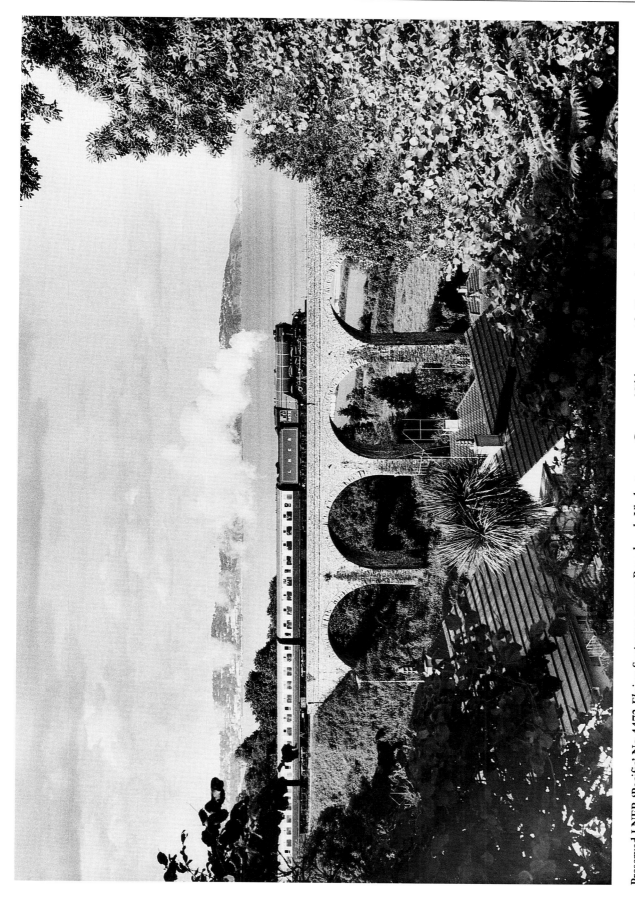

Preserved LNER 'Pacific' No 4472 *Flying Scotsman* crosses Broadsands Viaduct on the Paignton & Dartmouth Railway with an evening Paignton to Kingswear train on 22 July 1973. Notice how the viaduct, situated on the 1 in 60 climb towards Churston, is framed by the trees, and how the train stands out clearly against the waters of Torbay. Low evening sun highlights the train and viaduct.

Camera: Nikkormat with 50mm lens plus yellow filter. Exposure: 1/500th sec at f5.6. Film: Ilford FP4 rated at 125 ASA, developed in ID11 (undiluted).

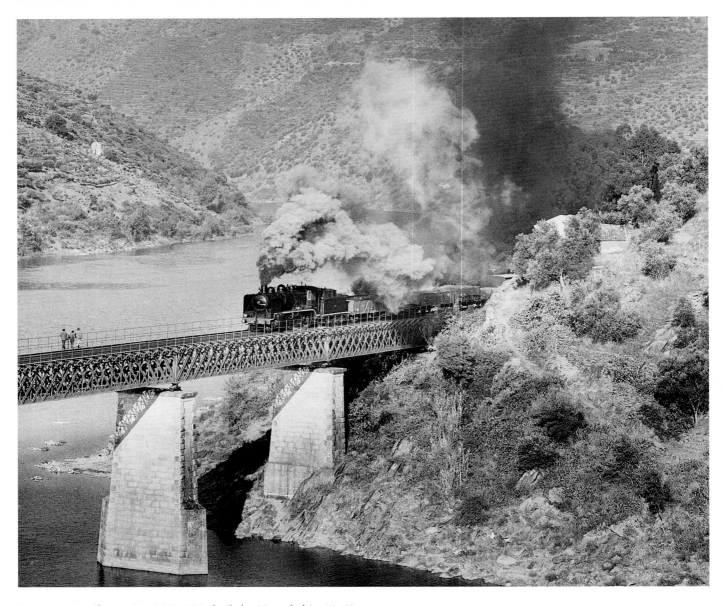

Portuguese Railways 4-6-0 No 291 (built by Henschel in 1913) crosses the junction of the River Tua and River Douro at Tua with a morning train from Regua bound for Barca D'Alva (near the Spanish border) on 23 September 1974. The locomotive here is a little above the Golden Section, but it was very important to include the foot of the pier where it met the river. In any case, the masonry columns looked so heavy that it was visually necessary to lift them clear of the bottom edge. These strongly contrasting features counterbalance the other three-quarters of the composition, which clearly show the fine variations in plant forms clinging to the mountain slopes. Some dramatic tension is developed by including the group of men using the catwalk as the engine approaches.

Camera: Nikkormat with 85mm lens plus yellow filter.
Exposure: 1/500th sec at f8. Film: Ilford FP4 rated at 200 ASA,
developed in Acuspecial.

Tunnels and deep cuttings

Generally locations around tunnels and deep cuttings are not as well lit as more open spaces, and as a result it is important to allow more exposure in these types of locations. The only circumstances when this may not be the case is when a location is so geographically placed that at certain times of the day it may be in full sunlight. It is important to take care when photographing steam locomotives around tunnels because of the problems that can be caused by the exhaust. If you are too near the mouth of the tunnel and the exhaust is excessive the point of the picture will be lost. In most circumstances it is better to let the train get well clear of the tunnel mouth, then shoot it.

The problems of photographing steam trains around tunnels and cuttings are emphasised in this picture of GWR pannier tank No 5764 emerging from Knowlsands Tunnel on the Severn Valley Railway with a Bewdley-Bridgnorth train on 10 August 1974. Note that the locomotive is well clear of the tunnel mouth, thus avoiding problems with lingering exhaust, etc.

As is so often the case in this type of location, lighting can present many exposure problems. This was particularly so in this case, where the sunlight was coming from the side and back. To overcome this problem it was necessary to give more exposure to the shadow areas (the front of the locomotive, etc) and burn in the highlights (the side of the train and the trees on the left-hand side) at the printing stage.

Camera: Nikkormat with 50mm lens plus yellow filter. Exposure: 1/500th sec at f5.6. Film: Ilford FP4 rated at 200 ASA, developed in Acuspecial.

Veteran 0-6-0 *Maude* hurries through Princes Street Gardens, Edinburgh, on 4 May 1980 with a special to Inverkeithing. This charming setting for an historic locomotive shows railway photography in its most delightful aspect. Although the cutting here is wider and lighter, it is still tree-lined, but the fresh budding branches form a perfect foil for the white exhaust, and while the tree trunks do grow out of the engine, they form such a consistent pattern that the eye accepts them as a texture; I only had to be careful to catch the chimney in a clear space. A few dark twigs in the top corner help to round off the picture and balance the darker engine. The raised viewpoint makes the rails slope more steeply and lends a sense of impatience as *Maude* gathers speed. The other diagonal comes from the steam, making an arrowhead shape with the track.

Camera: Nikkormat with 50mm standard lens plus yellow filter. Exposure: 1/250th sec at f4.5. Film: Ilford FP4 rated at 160 ASA, developed in Aculux.

On a lovely Autumn day, 7 October 1981, Midland Compound 4-4-0 No 1000 speeds south out of Harrogate with a special York circular train chartered by the Ford Motor Company. The vegetation in the cutting is most important, and the setting breaks down into distinct areas of texture, such as the willow herb in the lower left-hand corner, their middle greys making a perfect foil for the light and dark of the locomotive. The use of a yellow filter makes sure that the green trees in the cutting become light enough to make the darker locomotive stand out. Notice how the front of the boiler is further accentuated by catching it as it crosses a sunny patch of dry grass. Once again the high viewpoint gives the track a dynamic diagonal slope, while the engine is counterbalanced by the bridge and church steeple glimpsed through the trees.

Camera: Nikon FM with 50mm lens plus yellow filter.
Exposure: 1/500th sec at f8. Film: Ilford XP1 rated at 400 ASA, developed in XP1 chemicals.

Signals

The inclusion of semaphore signals invariably adds interest to any railway photograph. Indeed, there are many drab locations that have been transformed by this factor.

One way of enhancing any scene is to frame the train with signals, particularly if they are mounted on a large gantry. A good depth of field is obviously needed for success in these type of pictures, so that both signals and train are well in focus. The use of a standard or wide angle lens (obviously in conjunction good lighting conditions, enabling the use of smaller lens apertures) should not only ensure this, but is probably a necessity to include all of the signals and at the same time get a good balance on the train. If for physical reasons you do have to use a medium telephoto lens, it is most important to use as small an aperture (high f number) as possible, otherwise you will have too shallow a depth of field for satisfactory results. Also, because of their rapid demise the photographing of semaphore signals is in itself very important from an historical point of view, so it is always worthwhile taking them even if there is no train.

Colour-light signals, while not so attractive as semaphores, are very much part of today's railway scene and as such can be an integral part of any modern traction photograph. A low rear view of a train facing into a colour-light signal can be particularly effective in showing the signal aspect.

A very ordinary scene has been enhanced by the inclusion of semaphore signals, which, combined with good lighting and cloud effects, help to make a satisfying composition. The location is Burton Salmon, south of York on the Leeds line, and the train is a northbound passenger hauled by Brush Class 47 No 47279 on 24 May 1981.

Camera: Nikon FM with 50mm lens plus yellow filter.
Exposure: 1/1000th sec at f4.5. Film: Ilford FP4 rated at 160 ASA, developed in Aculux.

This is an obvious example of framing a train with a semaphore signal gantry, in this case at Falsgrave, outside Scarborough. The scene shows 'A3' 'Pacific' *Flying Scotsman* leaving the station with a special train for York on 26 August 1981.

Camera: Nikon FM with 50mm lens plus yellow filter. Exposure: 1/250th sec at f5.6. Film: Ilford XP1 rated at 400 ASA, developed in XP1 chemicals.

Stations

Most stations have an atmosphere all of their own, whether it be a cosy little country station with flower beds or a busy main-line station like York, with its wonderful roof and architecture and bustling crowds. Atmosphere is the key word in a station photograph, and somehow we have to convey this aspect.

Thus there are three basic ingredients in stations scenes – architecture, trains and human activity. The first two together will nearly always make satisfactory pictures providing that you get a balance between the train and the architecture, and that one does not cancel out the other. For example, if you are photographing at, say, a former GWR station, if you let the train obscure too much of the scene the picture will lose its identity and end up looking as though it could have been taken anywhere.

Human activity is all-important in station scenes, and in fact many fine pictures have been taken of only people. This is particularly so in big stations where people are involved in many different types of jobs that are all part of the railway environment, and naturally the passengers are also a vital ingredient of any station scene.

Add human activity to the first two ingredients – architecture and trains – and the combination should give you scope for many fine pictures. Concerning exposure, problems only really arise when photographing in covered stations, and great care must be taken to avoid underexposure.

With regard to what lenses to use for station scenes, this entirely depends on the location, but I would regard a combination of standard, short telephoto and medium wide angle lenses as sufficient for all types of pictures; indeed, a standard lens alone would get you by in most situations.

Left A pair of Class 5 4-6-0s, Nos 44477 and 45352, trundle through Snow Hill station on the evening of 12 August 1966. This picture illustrates a city station with its large number of tracks and spacious platforms, colour-light signals, over-all roof and canopies. In the distance, crowds can be seen waiting for arrivals and a period spotter can be seen on the left-hand side of the picture. The whole scene is overlooked by a typical city centre office block.

Camera: Konica 35mm range-finder with 45mm lens plus yellow filter. Exposure: 1/250th sec at f4. Film: Kodak Plus X rated at 125 ASA, developed in D76 (undiluted).

Above A sunny summer afternoon at St Austell station, Cornwall, as *Western Sovereign* pulls through with an up parcels train, passing another 'Western' diesel in an up loop with an empty stock train, on 8 August 1968. St Austell is a typical example of a former GWR country station with its splendid footbridge, station buildings and semaphore signals. Flower beds and surrounding trees complete the scene.

Camera: Konica range-finder with 45mm lens plus yellow filter. Exposure: 1/500th sec at f6.3. Film: Kodak Plus X rated at 125 ASA, developed in D76 (undiluted).

Above Isle of Man Railway 2-4-0 *Loch* pulls out of Douglas station on 31 August 1974 with the 2.15pm train to Port Erin. It is the people that help to bring this scene to life: notice how the line of the slope of the roof continues through the tilted cap of the driver and down to the object of his attention – the jet of steam from the cylinder cocks. The same line continues to the point lever on the left. This scene also captures the holiday spirit in the faces of the children on the right, eagerly watching the track ahead. The characteristic feature of these engines, the highly-polished brass dome, stands out clearly against a background of darker foliage.

Camera: Nikkormat with 35mm lens plus yellow filter.
Exposure: 1/500th sec at f6.3. Film: Ilford FP4 rated at
200 ASA, developed in Acuspecial.

Right A very different station in very different weather – this is Wolkenstein, Germany, and No 991 585, a Meyer 0-4-4-0 tank (75cm gauge) shunts in the station yard on 24 February 1981. This example of the 'starburst' structure shows the lines of perspective continuing invisibly from the top and bottom of the building and from the carriage on the left, towards the chimney of the locomotive; the confined space frames it perfectly. It was a bitterly cold day as can be seen from the exhaust, and the stark black shape of the building with its broken gutter accentuates the mood, as do the smashed windows on the left. This scene is made even more dramatic by the glimpses round the corner reflected in the carriage windows.

Camera: Nikon FM with 50mm lens plus yellow filter.
Exposure: 1/250th sec at f4. Film: Ilford FP4 rated at 160 ASA,
developed in Aculux.

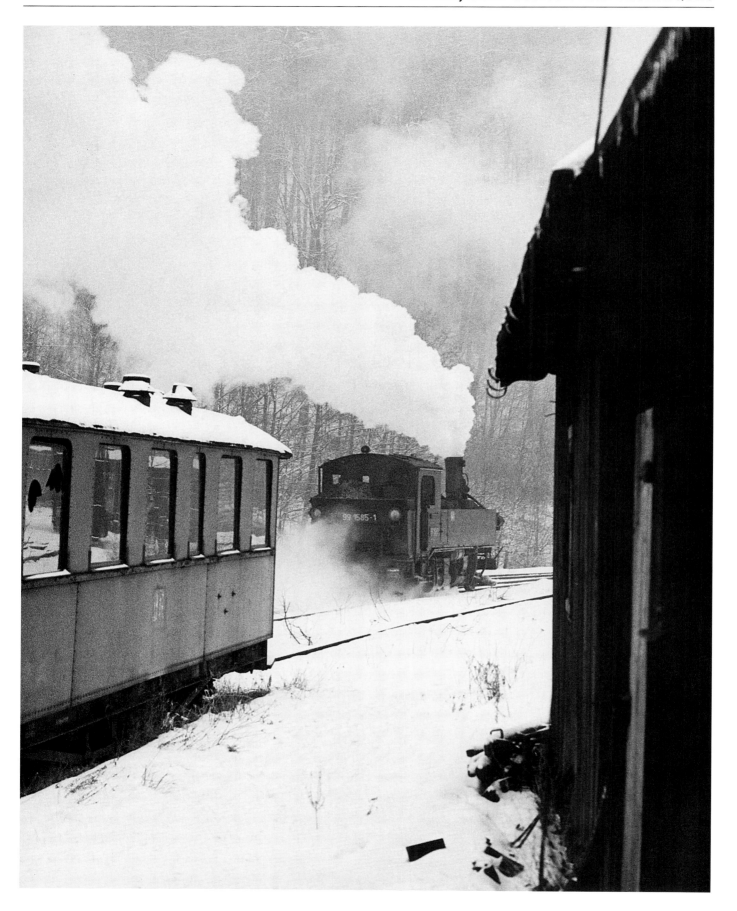

Sheds and depots

This type of photography can be divided into two distinct types: pictures taken inside sheds, usually of locomotives at rest, and activities in a shed yard, including watering, coaling, refuelling, maintenance, turning, etc.

For success in the first type of picture, because you will probably be working in a reasonably confined space it will be better to use a standard or medium wide angle lens, and in some cases, because there may be insufficient light, it will be necessary to use a tripod. If you do not have a tripod handy, try wedging yourself against a wall or post, which may help to steady your shot. I should add that since in this case you will be on railway property and will need a permit to be there, you should check that tripods will not cause a hazard to staff safety. As with all indoor photography, exposure can be a problem and it may well be worthwhile taking several shots of the same scene at different exposures.

Outdoor activity can provide plenty of scope and there are many opportunities to create atmospheric and evocative pictures. If available, a wide variety of lenses could be used to good advantage and experiment should be the order of the day. As with station photography, human activity can play an important part in shed photography and should not be overlooked.

Above Croes Newydd shed (Wrexham) on the afternoon of 13 March 1967 is the setting for this portrait of Standard Class 4 4-6-0 No 75002. Good lighting from the shed entrance (on the left) and sunlight from the roof combine to create beautiful patterns of light on the locomotive and its surroundings. Note the shadow of the chimney on the adjoining tender, and how the locomotive is framed by the foreground and roof. Great care was taken with the exposure for this picture, allowing plenty of exposure for the shadow areas (essential in this type of shot), while the highlights were burned in at the printing stage.

Camera: Konica range-finder with 45mm lens. Exposure: 1/60th sec at f4. Film: Kodak Plus X rated at 125 ASA, developed in D76 (undiluted).

Right On 25 February 1968 at Lostock Hall shed (Preston), Class 5 4-6-0 No 45345 receives admiring glances before moving off shed to Preston station to work the 5.52pm to Liverpool. Here is an example of the exception proving the rule where the Golden Section has been abandoned in favour of a dramatic imbalance. This increases the massive size of the locomotive against the tiny figures of the photographers. Notice how important is the man's raised arm, which follows the diagonal structure.

Camera: Konica range-finder with 45mm lens plus yellow filter. Exposure: 1/125th sec at f8. Film: Kodak Plus X rated at 125 ASA, developed in D76 (undiluted).

Above There is plenty of human (and animal) activity in this picture of Polish Class PX48 narrow gauge 0-8-0 No 1736 at Krosnewice shed, southern Poland, on 5 September 1975; it is interesting to note the method of coaling the locomotive.

Camera: Nikkormat with 50mm lens plus yellow filter.
Exposure: 1/250th sec at f5.6. Film: Ilford FP4 rated at
200 ASA, developed in Acuspecial.

Right At Cadley Hill Colliery, near Burton upon Trent, *Cadley Hill No 1*, a Hunslet 0-6-0, shunts at the exchange sidings on 25 May 1972. A warm day with diffuse lighting and little exhaust showing presents a challenge to every photographer. Fortunately I spotted this pattern of siding points that echoed the curve of the saddle tank, and by using a high viewpoint and medium telephoto lens I was able to make the tracks play an important part in this composition.

Camera: Nikkormat with 135mm lens plus yellow filter.
Exposure: 1/250th sec at f8. Film: Ilford FP4 rated at 200 ASA,
developed in Acuspecial.

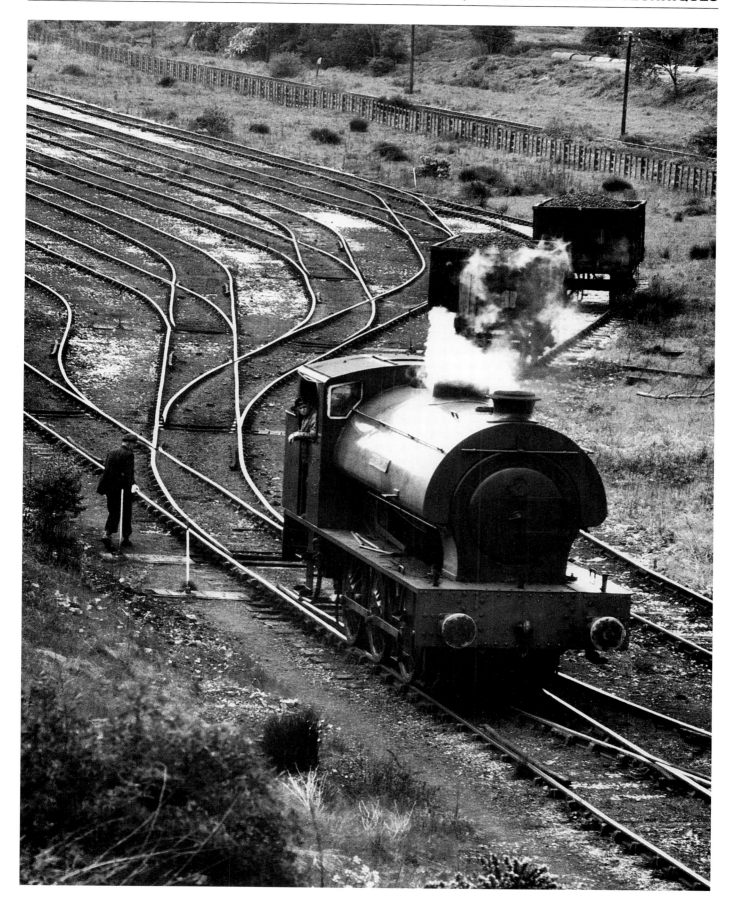

From the footplate and train

If you are lucky enough to get a rarely granted permit to ride on the footplate or cab of a locomotive, it is certainly worthwhile attempting to take photographs. The most popular type of picture from this position is surely the view from the cab window, and to get good results in these circumstances it is better to use a standard lens. This will give you a good depth of field and a fairly fast shutter speed to avoid camera shake, which is an obvious problem in a vibrating locomotive cab. Another type of shot is to show the men at work in the cab, and because of the confined space you will probably obtain better results by using a medium wide angle lens. Before taking any footplate picture try to adopt a firm stance, if possible by wedging your body against something solid, which will again help to reduce camera shake.

On some steam locomotives you will find a cab that is all 'bulled up', with the brightwork polished and sparkling. This can make a very attractive subject, especially in colour, but will be better if photographed when the locomotive is stationary; again you may find that a wide angle lens is very useful for this type of shot.

Photographing the locomotive from the carriage window of the train can also be very rewarding. Once again, a firm stance and fast shutter speed are prerequisites for satisfactory pictures. It is better to position yourself some way from the locomotive, around the middle to the rear of the train (depending on its length) and shoot when the train is on a tight curve. If you are a long way from the front of the train a medium telephoto lens might be ideal, but if you are not too far away a standard lens should suffice. From this position it is also possible to photograph oncoming trains on an adjoining track, but resist the temptation – it is highly dangerous.

Always have your camera handy when a train stops at a station because very often there will be a station scene or locomotive in front of your eyes that is worth photographing and you have only a split second to get your picture. A standard or wide angle lens should be the best lens for the job and it is in these circumstances that an automatic camera comes into its own.

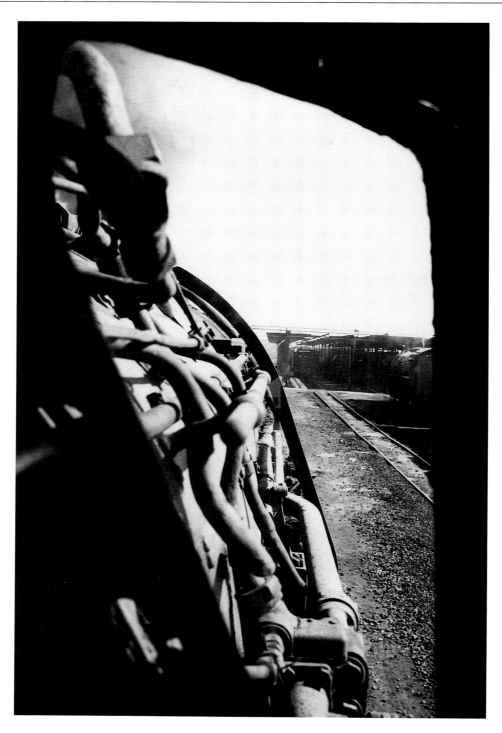

Left This picture was taken on the footplate of 0-6-0 saddle tank *Empress* at Cadley Hill Colliery on 23 November 1972. Note the shallow depth of field due to the use of a wide lens aperture, which in turn has focused attention on the driver. Also note the diagonal line from the driver's hand through to the yoke of his jacket, which adds energy to the picture.

Camera: Nikkormat with 50mm lens. Exposure: 1/500th sec at f2.8. Film: Ilford FP4 rated at 125 ASA, developed in ID11 (undiluted).

Above This view from the cab window of South African Railways Class GMA Garratt locomotive No 4064 was taken as it trundled through Capitol Park shed yard, Pretoria, on 20 July 1981. A shutter speed of 1/500th sec was necessary to avoid camera shake, and a standard lens at an aperture of f4 has given a reasonable depth of field.

Camera: Nikon FM with 50mm lens plus yellow filter. Exposure: 1/500th sec at f4. Film: Ilford Pan F rated at 50 ASA, developed in ID11 (undiluted).

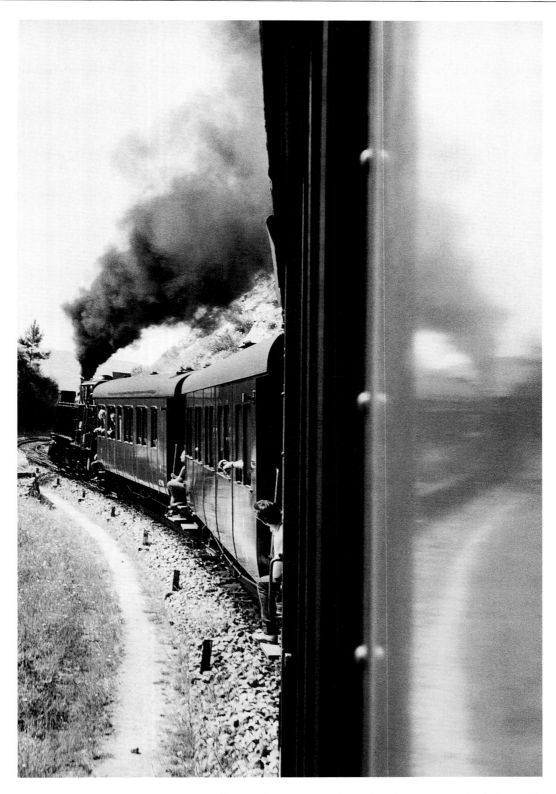

The tight curves usually found on narrow-gauge lines offer ample opportunity for this type of shot from a carriage window. The train is a special working from Regua to Chaves on the Portuguese metre-gauge system, hauled by Henschel 2-4-6-0 tank locomotive No E214 on 3 June 1969. The symmetry of the reflection is given extra interest by the carriage window frame being slightly off centre. Obviously a firm stance and grip is most important for this type of shot, meaning of course as fast a shutter speed as possible.

Camera: Konica range-finder with 45mm lens plus yellow filter. Exposure: 1/500th sec at f5.6. Film: Kodak Plus X rated at 125 ASA, developed in D76 (undiluted).

Panning and pacing

'Panning' is a way of creating the illusion of speed by catching a sharp image of a locomotive against a blurred background. The technique relies on swinging the camera round in the direction in which the train is travelling to match its speed as it passes, while using a shutter speed that is slow enough to show the rest of the scene as a blur. By using too fast a shutter speed, say 1/500th or 1/1000th sec, you will not only get a sharp engine but everything else will probably be sharp, which will ruin the pan effect.

How slow a shutter speed to choose depends primarily on the speed of the train. If it is moving fairly fast on a long straight, a shutter speed of 1/125th sec should be suitable. However, if it is only doing around 25mph, as on a preserved line perhaps, something around 1/30th sec should answer your needs. But remember that when using shutter speeds below 1/125th sec it is advisable to use a tripod to avoid camera shake. As the shutter speed you will be using will be slow, in most lighting conditions the aperture of the lens will therefore be small (high f number). It is therefore better to use a medium speed film when panning (around 100 ASA), for if you use too fast a film you may find that you will sometimes need a smaller aperture than your lens possesses. At this point it is also worth remembering that in poor lighting conditions, and when you only have a medium or slow speed film in your camera, panning is one way to get a good sharp picture of a locomotive that would otherwise be a blur.

Your choice of lens will depend on your location. As the ideal place to catch the locomotive is broadside on to you, you will need plenty of space along the line to give you room to stand back. Such spaces are to be found on multi-track lines and places such as demolished stations, or in open fields where the track is raised clear of the fence. It follows that if you are in a confined space a standard to medium wide angle lens is better, while if you are some distance away you may need a short telephoto lens. However, before choosing your lens it is important to find out the size of the locomotive, as a small tank engine takes up a fraction of the space of a large tender engine or main-line diesel locomotive. You must choose a location and lens that will let you capture the whole of the locomotive together with part of the leading carriage or wagon, and perhaps a third again to allow for misjudgement.

Focusing should not be too much of a problem because you know exactly where the locomotive is going to be and therefore can predetermine your focus setting. Also, because on most occasions you will be using smaller lens apertures (around f8 to f16), this will give you far greater depth of focus. However, remember that this depth of focus is greater on standard and wide angle lenses than on telephotos.

The technique of panning is to swing the camera round to match the speed of the train, firing the shutter when the locomotive is directly opposite you and framed in the viewfinder, but continuing to swing the camera while and after the shutter has been fired until the train is away from you. The most common mistake is 'targeting' the subject, instead of firing the shutter when the locomotive is fully side-on to you and across to the edge of the frame. In the excitement the shutter is fired when the camera is centred on the front of the locomotive, thus spoiling the pan. Practice first with a few dummy runs on passing cars.

Another mistake is in not matching the swing of the camera to the speed of the locomotive. This can take several forms, from weaving the lens up and down to jerking to a halt when the button is pressed. Practice makes perfect. Like a golfer, you must follow the swing through smoothly after making contact. This is when a tripod (used with a loose head) can be very useful, especially when you are using telephoto lenses, which are generally heavier than standard or wide angle lenses.

A more pronounced movement or blurring will be obtained from objects that are close to you and have a soft shape. The ideal location is a line running in front of a bank of trees or bushes. The sky is not much use as a background, as it has so little texture that the blurred effect will be lost. Sharply defined shapes such as telegraph poles are a problem as they spoil the horizontal streaks that create the flow of movement, and it is also difficult to judge the precise moment to photograph the train without finding a pole sticking up through the chimney.

The other technique is 'pacing' a train, that is panning from a vehicle that is moving at the same speed as the train, as, for example, from a car being driven on a long straight road without junctions parallel to the track. The same conditions apply here as with panning from a standing position, but because you are moving at the same speed as the train there is no need to swing the camera round with the train. Simply frame the subject and fire the shutter when it is side-on to you. Obviously you need a second person with you to drive the car, a clear road and the train moving at a low to medium speed. Under no circumstances should you attempt to drive and film at the same time, nor should it be attempted if other traffic is in the road, since in the excitement of the moment an accident can so easily be caused – and certainly it should not be attempted with a train travelling at express speeds.

In a car your main difficulty will be judging the best moment between telegraph poles and trees, as you cannot look ahead, only sideways. Your driver must warn you of such things as lineside features blocking the view, and the rise and fall of the road relative to the line. Be prepared to use a roll of film in order to get two or three decent shots, because you will need a considerable amount of luck to achieve a reasonable pacing shot.

One further point regarding shutter speeds: because you obviously cannot use a tripod inside a car, and with the movement of the car itself, it would be better to use a shutter speed of 1/125th sec, certainly no slower, and possibly 1/250th sec.

Panning and pacing are used deliberately to create the image of speed or possibly to salvage a good picture when

the light is failing. They can also be used to good advantage when a sideways view is the only reasonable one, such as when a steam locomotive is travelling tender-first. Another reason for panning might be when the landscape is not very photogenic, and reducing it to a blur makes up for its deficiencies. This technique can also be very useful when photographing modern traction, the impression of speed provided by a good pan shot making up for the lack of exhaust.

Class 'V2' 2-6-2 No 4771 *Green Arrow* is captured at speed south of York with a York Circular train on 25 June 1978. As the train was moving at around 50-60mph I was able to use a shutter speed of 1/125th sec and still get a blurred background. Also, a lens aperture of f8 ensured a good depth of field, thus avoiding any focusing problems.

Camera: Nikkormat with 50mm lens plus yellow filter.
Exposure: 1/125th sec at f8. Film: Ilford FP4 rated at 160 ASA, developed in Aculux.

Class 5 4-6-0 No 4767 nears Hexham with a train from Newcastle on 6 June 1981. This is a panned shot that has obviously been taken too soon. The position is wrong – I should have stood more to the left to allow the locomotive to clear the obscuring bush in the right foreground and the telegraph pole. Also, as the train was travelling at around 25-30mph, the shutter speed that I used (1/125th sec) was too fast; a speed of a 1/60th sec or even less was needed to blur the background and the wheels of the locomotive still further.

Camera: Nikon FM with 50mm lens plus yellow filter. Exposure: 1/125th sec at f8. Film: Ilford FP4 rated at 160 ASA, developed in Aculux.

Above Filmed from a car is South African Railways Class '25NC'
4-8-4 No 3525 at speed with a northbound goods on the famous
De Aar-Kimberley line at Houtkraal on 30 July 1982.

*Camera: Super Ikonta 6x6cm with 75mm lens. Exposure:
1/125th sec at f6.3. Film: Ilford FP4 rated at 125 ASA,
developed in ID11 (undiluted).*

Right A Birmingham-Kidderminster DMU enters Hagley station
on 28 October 1981. The GWR footbridge is a fine example of
railway architecture; notice the circular decorations bearing the
company's initials and the date of construction, 1884.

*Camera: Super Ikonta 6x6cm with 75mm lens. Exposure:
1/250th sec at f4. Film: Ilford FP4 rated at 125 ASA, developed
in ID11 (undiluted).*

Railway architecture

Stations are worth photographing for their own sake, whether or not a train is present. Old stations, richly decorated in the great metropolis or ornamented with simple rustic charm in the country, are all worth recording before they are modernised, and there are still treasures to be unearthed even on lines that have been abandoned. If nobody makes a record of them now, who will know what they looked like in a hundred years time?

Before the separate rail companies were nationalised under the name of British Railways, each company proudly stamped its signature with initials cast into the frames of seats and in roof brackets. The style of semaphore signals, whether upper or lower quadrant, and the design of signal boxes were often unique to the company that ran the line. Each company had its livery and colour scheme for paintwork, such as the light and dark stone of the Great Western, and each set of colours denoted the company's influence as surely as the capital letters woven into the design of the metal castings. Whenever a preserved line is used for a film sequence, the experienced eye will derive great pleasure from checking that the details are consistent!

Modern stations, although not so rich in detail, also have some photogenic features. The use of large areas of plate glass enables the photographer to see more different activities at the same time. Although familiarity dulls the powers of observation, we should try to record for posterity the most characteristic scenes of any period or event, such as the advertisements, the blackboard carrying notices of changes, the kind of people who use the services and the way they are dressed; for example, mini-skirts in profusion will date photographs to the late 1960s. Many photographs are brought to life when they include some human activity, and all these little details go to make your photographs something special. Once again a standard or medium wide angle lens would seem to be ideal for these type of pictures.

Maude, the preserved North British Railway 0-6-0 of 1888, poses for the camera at Blackburn station on the evening of 17 May 1980. It was on its way from the Scottish Railway Preservation Society at Falkirk to Rainhill for the Liverpool & Manchester 150th anniversary celebrations, and I caught sight of it waiting for a path, and recognised at once the potential of the scene. The station architecture plays an important role in the composition, the effectiveness of which relies on the repeating rhythms of the arches in the wall and the circular forms in the engine, such as the wheels, the dome, the name and headboard, and the banding on the boiler. This is definitely a picture for black and white film, and shows up the gloss of the paintwork against the texture of the sooty stone walls and the pattern of the rails. The four intervening tracks are compressed by the use of a short telephoto lens. The finishing touch comes from the jet of white steam, which relieves the blackness. Notice how the focus of interest, the driver and fireman, falls on the Golden Section and how the raised arm follows into the curve of the left-hand arch.

Camera: Nikon FM with 85mm lens plus yellow filter. Exposure: 1/250th sec at f5.6. Film: Ilford FP4 rated at 160 ASA, developed in Aculux.

6
Weather and lighting

Except when carried out in sheds, museums and some stations, railway photography is an outdoor pursuit and in consequence is at the mercy of all the elements and the problems that they can bring. In this chapter we shall deal with the different types of weather and lighting conditions that may be encountered and the technical problems that can arise from them.

Weather

Fog and mist
Because of the general lack of light in foggy and misty conditions, to obtain reasonable results it is essential to use a fairly fast film, certainly no less than 125 ASA and preferably around 400 ASA. As a general rule in these sort of conditions it is better to fill the frame with the locomotive and train rather than concentrating on landscape work. There are exceptions, especially in attractive settings, for example when a train is crossing a river, but in most such cases the train will probably appear as a semi-silhouette. One of the many problems encountered in foggy conditions is the lack of depth in the picture, but this can be countered to a certain extent by the use of a strong foreground such as a wall, hedge or clump of rocks. A certain amount of ingenuity is required to obtain good results in fog and mist and you will need to experiment.

Exposure is also a problem in these sorts of conditions (the day tends to look brighter than it actually is), and great care must be taken to avoid errors, especially in the case of underexposure. If you are not careful you will finish up with such a thin negative that is almost impossible to print to a reasonable standard, and, if you are using colour reversal film, a transparency that is too dark for any sort of projection.

Having said all this, pictures taken on misty days, especially of steam at work, have an atmosphere of their own, and some very satisfying compositions can be obtained in these conditions.

Rain
Rain can certainly be a hazard to the railway photographer, especially in Britain, where we seem to have more than our fair share! But what is usually a disadvantage can sometimes turn things to our advantage. This is especially so on a dull day, when the advent of rain can add much sparkle to an otherwise drab scene. The metal of the rails glistens, locomotives and trains can take on a very shiny and photogenic appearance, and exhausts hang in the air, while puddles on platforms bring opportunities for reflections, so do not give up because it is raining – you may be more than a little surprised with the results. However, remember to take a good strong umbrella to keep yourself and your equipment dry, and if possible have someone with you who can hold the umbrella – spouses and partners please note!

When it rains really hard, larger stations can usually provide a certain amount of cover under which to operate to avoid getting very wet. This is worth bearing in mind when you want to photograph an important train and the weather bars you from more open locations.

Wind
Wind is not a problem when photographing diesel and electric traction, but is certainly a serious hazard as far as steam is concerned. Many fine steam shots have been spoiled because of strong wind causing the exhaust to blow over the side of the engine and obscure it in 'clag'. This is especially so if wind and sunlight are coming from opposite directions. The most practical thing to do in these circumstances is to take the picture from as low an angle as possible (if practical, from below rail level); by doing this, and with a bit of luck, you may get a decent picture with the exhaust just clear of the train, but this is not always the case and you may have many failures. The other alternative is to take the picture against the light – in other words create a silhouette, a technique discussed later on in this chapter.

Of course, if the sun is not out you can take your picture from the windward side, which will effectively obviate any problems. But 'Murphy's Law' being what it is, with strong winds you inevitably get sunshine from the opposite side, and even blustery winds can momentarily change direction and cause the exhaust to swirl.

A pair of German narrow-gauge Meyer 0-4-4-0 tank engines, Nos 99 1561 and 99 1585, leave Wolkenstein for Johstad with a freight consisting of standard-gauge wagons on transporters on 24 February 1981. Although because of the misty conditions the train appears as a semi-silhouette, the attractive setting compensates for the lack of detail. Note also how in these cold and damp conditions the exhausts of the locomotives cling in the air.

Camera: Nikon FM with 50mm lens plus yellow filter. Exposure: 1/500th sec at f4. Film: Ilford FP4 rated at 160 ASA, developed in Aculux.

The conditions when I took this picture were pretty appalling – torrential rain! However, thanks to my wife who held the umbrella I was able to achieve a satisfying picture. The rain has added sparkle to the rails and sleepers, rooftops and bushes, and has highlighted the locomotive and train, while the damp conditions have also meant good steam effects. As the lighting conditions were dull (the exposure was a 1/250th sec at f3.5 using 400 ASA film), I used a medium wide angle lens to obtain greater depth of field. The location is the entrance to Standedge Tunnel on the Diggle route and the train is the SLOA 'Trans Pennine Pullman' hauled by Class 5 4-6-0 No 5305 on 26 September 1981.

Camera: Nikon FM with 35mm lens. Exposure: 1/250th sec at f3.5. Film: Ilford XP1 rated at 400 ASA, developed in XP1 chemicals.

Above The disastrous effect of wind on steam locomotives is well illustrated in this picture of Nos 5000 and 80079 north of Church Stretton with a special train on 19 April 1980. As the sun and wind were coming from opposite sides, nothing could really have been done about this except hope that the wind would drop for a few seconds enabling me to achieve a successful picture, but obviously the gamble did not pay off. In fact, I took around a dozen pictures (using a motor drive) of this scene and every one was in my opinion a disaster.

Camera: Nikon FM with 85mm lens plus yellow filter.
Exposure: 1/500th sec at f6.3. Film: Ilford FP4 rated at
160 ASA, developed in Aculux.

Snow

Snow and sunshine can be a bonus to the railway photographer because railway snow scenes, particularly when you add sunshine, can be among the most beautiful and atmospheric pictures that it is possible to obtain – always assuming that the weather does not stop the trains, or your ability to reach a suitable location.

The greatest problem that snow brings is the one of assessing the correct exposure. When photographing in the snow take a meter reading for the snow area and one for

Right Sunshine and snow invariably form the basis for attractive railway photographs, as can been see from this shot of a Longbridge-bound DMU as it approaches the University station in the suburbs of Birmingham on 8 December 1981. On the right-hand side is the Worcester-Birmingham Canal. In calculating the exposure for this picture, I took a reading for the snow area, which was around f11 at 1/500th sec, and a reading for the surrounding bushes, which was f5.6 at 1/500th sec. I assumed that the reading for the bushes would be similar to that of the train, and 'bracketed' the two exposures, deciding that an aperture of around f6.3 would give me a reasonably correct exposure. Highlights were burned in at the printing stage.

Camera: Nikon FM with 50mm lens plus yellow filter.
Exposure: 1/500th sec at f6.3. Film: Ilford XP1 rated at
400 ASA, developed in XP1 chemicals.

the main subject, if static; if it is an action shot, estimate the exposure for the train, remembering that it will be much darker than the snow and will require far more exposure. Then use a compromise between the different readings. If there is a wide difference, always err on the side of the main subject. For example, if you have a 400 ASA film in the camera, meter readings might be 1/500th sec at f8-f11

On days when it is actually snowing, the lighting factors are similar to those in fog and mist. The engine appears as a semi-silhouette, and the landscape recedes into paler shades of grey. But where snow lies on the ground it gives extra lightness to otherwise sombre areas, and of course where it clings to branches, fences, etc, it brings a sparkling dimension of textures to the picture, as shown in the previous photograph. However, the bushes and sheds here at West Cannock Colliery, Staffs, on 19 December 1969 are still dark and serve to show up the driving snowflakes, increasing the wintry feeling. The use of a fast film with its conspicuous grain adds to this effect. Notice how the angles of the exhaust and the rough verges lead the eye to the locomotive, Bagnall 0-6-0 saddle tank *Topham*, helped by the man walking towards it.

Camera: Konica range-finder with 45mm lens. Exposure: 1/250th sec at f4. Film: Kodak Tri-X rated at 400 ASA, developed in D76 (undiluted).

for the snow area, and 1/500th sec at f5.6 for the train. Therefore set the lens to an aperture of f6.3 (still at 1/500th sec for the shutter), which exposure should give you plenty of detail in the main subject and not too much overexposure in the snow area. However, a word of warning: it is all right to have a certain amount of overexposure when using negative film in these weather conditions, but when you are using colour reversal film in adverse conditions like snow, it is probably better to stick to the general meter reading, which will give you a slightly darker and perhaps more dramatic slide but, more important, one that will retain more detail in the highlights. Moreover, with sun on snow the darker parts of the train will be bottom-lit with light reflected off the snow.

When blizzard conditions prevail you really need a dark background to emphasise the driving snow. One idea is to photograph a train as it emerges from beneath a bridge – if you set it against the sky you will tend to lose the effect of the falling snow.

When out in this sort of weather always wrap up warmly and take an umbrella as protection for you and your equipment. While dealing with the protection of equipment in extremely cold weather, to avoid things like shutter and battery failure keep your camera as warm as possible, either in a camera gadget bag or case or even inside your jacket.

Lighting

In the chapter on equipment we discussed the lens aperture or iris, which controls the amount of light that enters the camera, the size of the opening being indicated by the 'f' number. The lower the f number, say f1.8, the more light is allowed in, and the higher the f number, say f16, the less light is allowed in. So when we talk about overexposing by one stop on a meter reading, we mean using a lower f number, and the opposite in the case of underexposure. For example:

Meter reading = 1/250th sec at f8
One stop overexposure = 1/250th sec at f5.6
One stop underexposure = 1/250th sec at f11

The same effect can be obtained by adjusting the camera shutter speed and keeping the aperture static at f8 To overexpose by one stop you would use the next slower shutter speed (1/125th sec) and to underexpose by one stop the next higher (1/500th sec). If you wish to overexpose or underexpose by two stops, you must alter

This picture of 'Western' Class diesel No D1048 *Western Lady* with a Birmingham-Paddington train near Harbury on 17 April 1976 is a good example of even lighting with no really dense shadow to present exposure problems. The light reading used was that taken for the whole scene without any adjustment.

Camera: Nikkormat with 50mm lens plus yellow filter. Exposure: 1/500th sec at f5.6. Film: Ilford FP4 rated at 160 ASA, developed in Aculux.

Here the sun is on the front of the locomotive, but unavoidably is coming from the opposite side of the line from the camera, so the side of the train is in shadow. I allowed extra exposure for this when taking the photograph, and at the printing stage held back the shadow area to retain more detail. The train is the 11.43 York to King's Cross hauled by 'Deltic' No 55016 *Gordon Highlander* and the location is Selby swing bridge on 24 May 1981.

Camera: Nikon FM with 85mm lens plus yellow filter. Exposure: 1/500th sec at f4.5. Film: Ilford FP4 rated at 160 ASA, developed in Aculux.

the shutter speed either down or up by two speeds, and so on. This last method may be more useful on occasions, certainly when taking stills, to allow a higher aperture f number to be used, giving greater focal length.

Normal lighting

By normal lighting we simply mean even lighting, and this comes in two major categories. The first is when there is no clear sunlight and virtually everywhere has an evenness of light about it from continuous cloud cover. The second category is when there is bright sunlight and you are taking the photograph with the sun behind you; the whole scene is more or less evenly illuminated by the sun, without the dense shadows and extreme contrast provided by side lighting.

In both of these situations exposure should not present a problem and straightforward meter readings of the main scene will probably suffice for reasonably accurate exposures resulting in good negatives and transparencies. The only thing to be careful of is when photographing a dark or black locomotive, particularly in colour. In these

circumstances it would to prudent to overexpose slightly and open up the lens by half to one stop (use a lower f number) to obtain maximum detail in the main subject, the locomotive.

There are occasions when, although you have the sunlight on the front of the subject, you are physically unable to take the photograph from the sunny side, and in consequence the side of the subject is in shadow. Providing that the shadow area is not too dense, it is still possible to get a satisfactory picture by allowing extra exposure for the shadow area. This is especially so if you are using black and white film, but does not always work out as well with colour film because of the obvious loss of colour in the subject (shadow) area.

Side and back lighting

Side lighting is when you take a photograph with the sun roughly at right angles to the line of vision of your camera, creating strong highlights and shadows. Back lighting is provided when that angle is even more extreme, perhaps only illuminating the details of the edges of the subject (see the picture on page 22). This type of lighting can be used to best advantage when the sun is low in the sky, especially early in the morning and late in the afternoon. The effect of side and back lighting is to throw the subject into strong relief, and this is very apparent when photographing hard-edged metallic subjects like locomotives and trains. The use of a lens hood is a must when photographing in this type of lighting to avoid any flare on the lens, and it is important to position the camera so that the sun is not actually shining into the lens.

The lighting in this picture is opposite from the previous one. The front of the locomotive is in shadow, with full sunlight on the side. However, as in the previous picture, extra exposure was given for the shadow area, and at the printing stage the shadow area was held back and the highlights were burned in. The scene shows 0-6-0 diesel shunter No 08068 at work at Bromford Bridge sidings, Birmingham, on 14 April 1982.

Camera: Nikon FM with 135mm lens plus yellow filter. Exposure: 1/500th sec at f6.3. Film: Ilford XP1 rated at 400 ASA, developed in XP1 chemicals.

Silhouette at Waterside in south-west Scotland as Barclay 0-4-0 saddle tank No 21 shunts on a tip near Dunaskin Colliery on 30 August 1973. By using the exposure given by the light meter for the sky, I deliberately underexposed for the engine, rendering it as an almost black shape. This gave me the chance to show off the dramatic exhaust and cloud formations. Also, by choosing a low viewpoint, I could hide any intruding trees that might detract from this simple composition. The foreground is relieved by the shiny facets of coal, which would otherwise be too heavy and black.

Camera: Nikkormat with 35mm lens plus yellow filter. Exposure: 1/500th sec at f8. Film: Ilford FP4 rated at 200 ASA, developed in Acuspecial.

Obviously when the sun is low the shadows are longer and can form a dramatic part of the composition. But this in turn creates some exposure problems. It is very important to retain a certain amount of detail in the shadow area, otherwise you will finish up with shadows that are far too dense and contrasty.

This is very pronounced in monochrome work, the results being known in the trade as 'soot and whitewash' prints. Great care must therefore be taken with exposure. Try working on an exposure that is a balance between the light reading for the shadow area and for the highlights. This applies equally well when working with colour negative film, but when using transparency film in these types of lighting conditions it is best to avoid too much overexposure because you may finish up with washed-out highlights. It is far better on a slide to have slightly denser and perhaps more dramatic shadows but to retain good detail in the highlights.

Silhouette

Basically a silhouette effect is created when you shoot the locomotive or train (or any another principal subject of the picture) totally against the light to create a black or very dark profile set against a light background, preferably a dappled sky or rippling water for maximum effect. Such photographs certainly have impact and are equally effective when using either colour or black and white film.

The technique required for this type of picture is not at all difficult because all you really do is place the subject between the camera and light source. Take a meter reading for the background (that is, the light source) and expose for this. It should completely underexpose the foreground and main subject, rendering them with very little if any detail on the negative or transparency and in consequence creating the desired silhouette effect.

The maximum impact can be obtained when there is low evening or morning sun, but if you film against the light when the sun is high, even in silhouette work, be careful to shield the lens from the rays of the sun or you will finish up with far too much flare, which will tend to spoil the overall effect.

A tremendous silhouette effect can often be obtained when filming a train crossing a bridge, particularly if it is of the lattice girder type. Film from as low an angle as possible to create maximum effect.

Look out for the silhouette shot. You may be in a very ordinary location, but by simply changing your position and shooting against the light you may well create a 'master shot'.

7
Night photography

An important aspect of railway photography, and one that is so often neglected by the enthusiast, is photographing the railway scene at night. Night has much to offer the cameraman, especially at a large station, which looks entirely different when lit from within. This also applies to locomotive depots, where the juxtaposition of locomotives can create many unusual contrasts, and of course the steam locomotive at night can take on a dragon-like glow – firelight fills the cab and picks out the faces of the crew, while sparks fountain up from the chimney and coals flicker with blue flames as the ashpan is raked out.

It is important to bear in mind that rail traffic is different at night. At large stations mail and newspaper trains are either being loaded or unloaded (giving ample time for time exposures) and platforms are usually quite barren of passengers. At this point it is prudent to mention that you should have either a platform or travel ticket; even if a platform ticket is not required (as is the case at some open stations), for security reasons let someone in authority know of your presence and what you plan to do. With regard to locomotive depots, you will require written permission before visiting them. An important safety factor is that you should wear something white or reflective and carry a pocket torch, which will be very useful for changing films, timing exposures, checking apertures, etc.

There are two main ways of undertaking night photography, using a flashlight and taking pictures by available light (usually known as time exposure).

Flashlight

Flash guns are generally used for night shots. Today a frequent example is when a special train has returned and is waiting for its passengers to alight before the locomotive goes to shed. The locomotive is usually surrounded by enthusiasts, but if you are patient you can sometimes find a few seconds when the crowd pulls back and gives you a clear view of the engine. It is better to photograph from behind the crowd, looking at the backs of their heads, because otherwise their faces show up in flashlight as very pale patches that might upset the balance of your

composition. In any case, nobody enjoys having a flash gun dazzling their eyes, especially the driver. You must not, incidentally, fire off a flash unit towards the cab of a moving train, as this could temporarily blind the driver, which could have dangerous consequences.

Another situation where flashlight photography is useful is where a locomotive is standing on a track surrounded by poles and wires, etc. In daylight these would present such a cluttered appearance that your shot of the engine would be unacceptable. But at night all these unwanted features will be lost in the darkness, while the locomotive will show up clearly silhouetted, pale against the black. Here, flash is better than an available light picture, where the poles might appear in your shot.

Some people use flash in very dull or gloomy daylight conditions, such as under station canopies. In these circumstances the flash gun helps to fill in very heavy shadows. It also makes painted surfaces seem to be more glossy and adds sparkle to the fittings. This is because the source of light is a comparatively small point, unlike the sky, and any curved shiny surfaces will reflect this as more definite lines and points of light. This makes the locomotive stand out more brightly in its setting.

Most cameras are fitted with a 'hot-shoe' into which the flash unit fits. In this position, by means of a contact on the

A night study of former Somerset & Dorset 2-8-0 No 13809 at York on 24 October 1981 after working in with a special train. Because of the number of people around the locomotive this was an instance where it would have been impossible to have used a time exposure. I settled instead for a portrait of the front end of the locomotive, partly because of the people but also because of the very dark available lighting conditions (the locomotive was at the end of the platform and away from all the main station lighting). The use of a medium wide angle lens enabled me to move in fairly close to the subject, an obvious advantage with flash photography, and gave greater depth of field. The flash was held to the right of the camera and gives just a suggestion of shadow to such details as headlamp and buffers.

Camera: Nikon FM with 35mm lens. Exposure: 1/125th sec with electronic flash at Nikon FM setting of f4. Film: Ilford XP1 rated at 400 ASA, developed in XP1 chemicals.

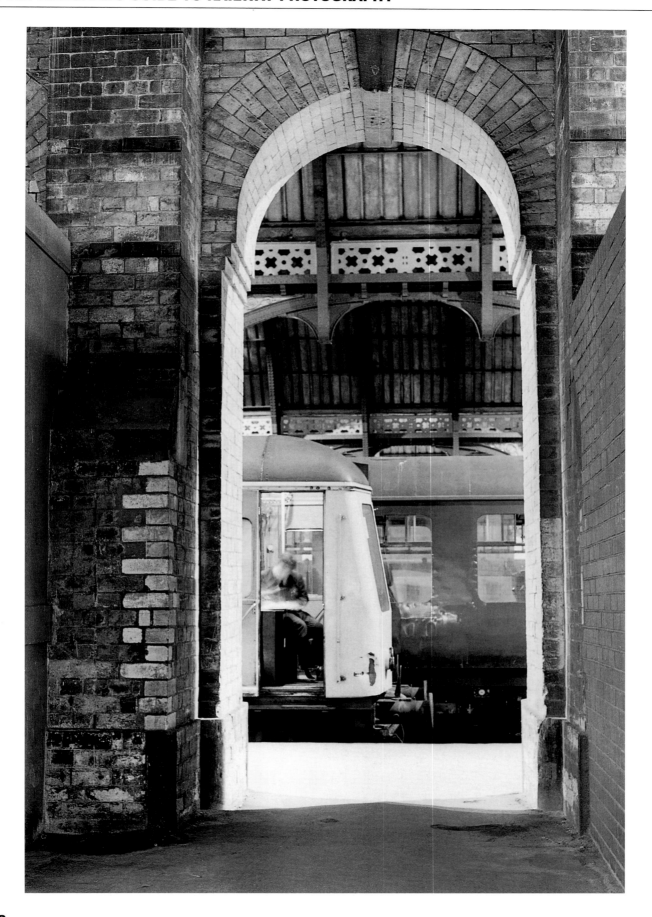

This vignette of station architecture at York on 30 August 1981 relies on a fairly small aperture and a longish 45-second time exposure to keep as much of the view in focus as possible. The only blurred shape is the driver of the DMU sorting through his paperwork. However, because the general level of illumination was good and the direction of light was so similar to that of daylight, the photo loses the character of a night shot, which is usually a subject well-lit from a low source against a dark background. On the plus side, the framing arch could only have been equally lit by artificial light.

On these low light readings an ordinary meter is not reliable, because of 'reciprocity failure', ie the normal equivalents of shutter and aperture settings in the middle range of daylight do not hold true at the extreme ends of the scale. It is possible to use a specialist cadmium-sulphide meter for accurate low readings, but for general use experience and 'bracketing' the exposure should suffice.

Camera: Nikon FM with 35mm lens. Exposure: 45 sec at f8.
Film: Ilford XP1 rated at 400 ASA, developed in XP1 chemicals.

hot-shoe, the flash unit will fire simultaneously with the camera shutter. Most cameras (with the exception of those that have leaf shutters fitted into their lenses) will have a shutter speed recommended for flash work, which you must use. If you set a faster speed you will end up with part of each frame blanked out.

It is possible to fire the flash gun independently of the hot-shoe. Some cameras have a way of extending the circuit, synchronising the flash by a lead that plugs into the front of the camera. The camera can then be fired with one hand and the flash with the other. The advantage of this system is that you can separate the direction of the light from the angle of the camera's view. The light, coming from a different angle, will cast shadows on the subject that the camera will be able to see, but would not be able to do so if the flash was mounted on top of the camera. The shadows help to show up the shape of the locomotive in relief, which could make an interesting picture.

Your flash equipment, whether bulb or electronic, should have instructions indicating how many times the bulbs can be used, or roughly how many exposures the batteries will give you in your electronic flash. It is also important when using electronic flash to have some idea of the re-cycling time required between each flash shot.

Most flash units are fitted with calculators (some are computerised) so that you can determine which aperture (f stop) to use. This is calculated by the speed of the film and the distance from the subject. For example, if you are using a film with a speed of 50 ASA and you are 20-30 feet away from your subject, this should enable you to use an aperture of around f3.5 and obtain a reasonable exposure. Simple flash calculators made of card can be obtained from photographic shops, or are sometimes given away with photographic magazines.

Such calculators are for use primarily indoors where the light source is fairly constant, but outdoors it is a different matter. A black-fronted steam locomotive will require more exposure than a yellow-fronted diesel. Thus in practice, although exposures are determined by calculators, you will need to experiment and make a careful note of your exposures to see which gives you the best results. Your first attempts will tell you a lot, and you will develop an instinct for what is possible.

When you buy an electronic flash unit primarily for use in railway photography, it is more important to buy a unit that will give you as much depth of light as possible, rather than one that has all the latest gadgets (important as these may be). If you can afford a flash unit that has everything, so much the better.

Available light

When a locomotive or train is stationary you can take a picture using available light. By keeping the shutter of your camera open for a long time, even minutes, you should be able to achieve a satisfactory negative or transparency. These are known as time exposures. Most cameras have the symbol 'B' at the slow end of the shutter speed scale, standing for 'bulb' (originally shutters were operated by squeezing a bulb), and at this setting the shutter will stay open as long as the shutter button is pressed. To avoid any movement of the camera during the exposure you will need to mount the camera on a firm tripod and depress the shutter by a cable release that will lock in the depressed position. If you do not have a tripod and cable release and there is enough light to take your shot within the timed shutter settings (some of today's cameras have very slow shutter speeds) you can avoid camera shake by lodging the camera securely on a firm surface and winding back the 10-second delay lever (self-timer), then fire the shutter at the required speed. This means that the shutter will be fired independently after 10 seconds, thus cutting out shake caused by your finger depressing the shutter button. This can work out well in an emergency, and provided the camera is fitted with a self-timer, but it is better to use a tripod and cable release if possible.

Wind can be another hazard. Try to find something to act as a windbreak to prevent your camera being vibrated or, worse still, blown over. On rough ground try to bed the legs of the tripod into the earth and stamp the soil firm.

When it is raining you will need to shelter your camera with, if possible, an umbrella. Check the lens before each exposure for drops of water on the surface and wipe dry with a clean cotton handkerchief that will not leave any

Midland Compound 4-4-0 No 1000 poses at Carlisle Upperby on the bitterly cold winter's night of 11 February 1983. This classic three-quarter front portrait is given greater power and elegance by the low viewpoint of the camera on a tripod. The boiler towers over the photographer, rising in dynamic diagonals, while the lens, being closer to the ground, picks out the details of the wheels. This low angle also makes the locomotive cover up any unwanted poles that otherwise would spoil the profile.

The lighting conditions were most exciting – and demanding – as it was very dark, the only sources of illumination being a lamp behind the boiler and the gleam of the snow. As the locomotive was a black silhouette, I used about five 'fill-in' flashes along the side and three from one spot at the front to build up more light.

Camera: Nikon FM with 35mm lens. Exposure: 1½ min at f8 with fill-in flash. Film: Ilford XP1 rated at 400 ASA, developed in XP1 chemicals.

fluff on the glass. On foggy nights and in the small hours you may find condensation a problem, but frequent cleaning with the cloth should help.

Your next challenge will be judging the length of exposure. As every station and depot will have a different light intensity, inspired guesswork and experiment should help to solve the problem. If possible it is better to take two or three shots of the same subjects at various exposures, known as 'bracketing' the exposures. If you keep the lens aperture at around f8 to f16 (depending on the length of your lens – the longer the lens the higher the f number) and focus on a point, say, 30 feet from your camera, then from around 15 feet to infinity should be in focus. In other words, remain on a fixed aperture and vary your shutter speeds, for example 20 seconds at f11, 40 seconds at f11, and 60 seconds at f11. Time exposures at night really are guesswork, but persevere (remembering to make a note of all exposures) and some quite startling results can be obtained.

Another useful idea when you are shooting time

exposures is to 'paint in' the subject with a flash gun. Use a very long exposure on a stationary subject that is very poorly lit, and leave the camera's shutter open for a fair length of time, thus allowing you time to let off a flash gun near the subject to 'fill in'. However, you must be careful to hide yourself when you let off the flash or your image may be registered on the film. After firing the flash, if there is time move on to another point of the subject and repeat the process.

As for the right lens to use for night photography, obviously telephoto lenses are out, but apart from using the standard lens it is well worthwhile considering using a wide angle lens. With a medium wide angle lens you are able to get closer to the subject, which is very useful when you are using flash. Also, because a wide angle gives a greater depth of field compared to a standard lens, it may help with any focusing problems encountered in night photography. Railway photography at night is a challenge, but one that can also be very rewarding and enjoyable.

On the evening of 30 October 1984 a pair of English Electric Class 50 locomotives pose side by side at Exeter St David's station; on the left is No 50010 *Monarch* waiting to leave with the 19.34 to Waterloo, and on the right is No 50012 *Benbow* on the 15.40 Birmingham New Street to Penzance train. Compared to the picture on page 112, this is obviously a night shot with low light sources and a dark sky. Note the position of the station lights, as well as the headlights of the locomotives, which all add sparkle to the picture. The cab shapes also echo the shapes of the platform canopies.

Camera: Nikon FM with 50mm lens. Exposure: 75 sec at f8.
Film: Ilford XP1 rated at 400 ASA, developed in XP1 chemicals.

8
Common faults
and remedies

Fault: Picture out of focus. The background is sharp but the locomotive in the foreground is blurred.

Remedy: Nothing can be done about a photograph that is out of focus. Always take very great care when focusing, but if the problem persists have your camera checked by a reliable repairer.

Fault: Too slow a shutter speed. The ballast and track under the locomotive are fairly sharp but the moving train is blurred.

Remedy: Light permitting, always use a shutter speed that is fast enough to 'freeze' the movement of the train. If lighting conditions do not permit this, if possible take the train more head-on to slow the relative horizontal movement.

Above Fault: Camera shake. The whole of the picture is blurred through attempting to take a still shot, hand-held, at far too slow a shutter speed (in this case l/8th sec), which has caused camera shake.

Remedy: For this type of shot, where a slow shutter speed is required, always use a tripod and cable release. The only other way is to steady your body against something firm and hope that this will give a sharp picture.

Below Fault: Parapet of bridge included in shot. As many pictures are taken from this type of location, this could be a recurring problem, especially if you use a range-finder camera where the picture in the viewfinder is slightly higher than the lens. Remember also that even with single lens reflex cameras the field of vision is not 100 per cent of the picture that the camera is taking.

Remedy: Always take greater care to check that you have allowed enough clearance. One remedy is to raise your height by standing on something.

Above Fault: Objects protruding from top of locomotive and train.

Remedy: When filming in this type of location, either photograph from a lower angle in order to let the train cover the background, or from a much higher angle (in this case the station footbridge) in order to separate the train from the background, or provide a positive background.

Below Fault: Tender-first locomotive too head-on.

Remedy: Never take a tender or bunker-first locomotive from this angle unless you want to finish up with a picture of a tender or bunker, which are not really photogenic – unless you are after an 'operating' picture to show this type of working. Instead, choose a location with great care to ensure as much of a side view of the locomotive and train as possible.

Above Fault: Subject taken too early, too far away and picture tilted.
Remedy: Let the locomotive and train fill the frame without
running out of it and look for the significant verticals/horizontals
in order to align the picture correctly. Here, the hill on the skyline
provides a false horizontal. Remember also that while telegraph
poles and fence posts should be vertical but might not be,
buildings and structures ought to be.

Below Fault: Flash picture taken at wrong shutter speed for
camera, and picture tilted.
Remedy: Always make sure that the shutter of your camera is set
on the correct speed setting for flash photography. These vary
with different makes of camera – on some they are 1/80th sec, on
others 1/125th sec, and so on. Make sure the camera is aligned,
as described above.

Left Fault: Not winding on sufficient frames at beginning of film causes partial fogging of first frame (35mm only).
Remedy: Simply wind on an extra frame at the beginning of the film – better to lose a frame than ruin a picture.

Below left Fault: Photographer's own shadow in picture, a problem that can arise in early morning or late evening and is easily overlooked.
Remedy: Watch where you are standing, and alter the angle if possible. The shadow can be cut out at the printing stage (if using black and white or colour negative film), and colour transparencies can be masked, but in both instances this may spoil the balance of the picture. Another solution would be (if possible) to use a longer lens and thus cut out the shadows at source.

Fault: Lens cap not removed.
Remedy: !!!!

9
General information

This section deals with the more general aspects of railway photography not covered in previous chapters, but which are nevertheless very important, not only in regard to railways but also to photography in general.

Keeping records

This is an important but fairly simple thing to do, but one that is often overlooked by photographers. The best way I have found of keeping records is to note down each shot as you take it. I use two sets of notebooks, one set for black and white and the other for colour, and separate books for different subjects, ie British Railways (diesel and steam), overseas, industrial, etc. Each film is numbered BR 24, O 32, IND 14, and so on.

As well as the obvious things to record, such as the date, locomotive number, location, etc, it is as well, particularly with black and white films, to make a note of the film speeds, shutter speeds, apertures and conditions. These things can be useful later on, especially at the printing stage, allowing the best negatives to be selected (see Figure 6). For example, with negatives of similar pictorial content but taken at different shutter speeds and apertures (which can happen, especially when chasing a train), a shot taken at a 1/500th at f6.3 will nearly always be sharper than one taken at a 1/250th at f4. This is not always apparent, even when the negative is blown up in the enlarger (before the print is made), and it is sometimes only on the final print that any deficiencies become obvious. This information could save time and materials. An example of record book layout is shown below.

Storing films and prints

Negatives

After developing a roll of film, cut the film into strips of six for 35mm or four for larger negative sizes, then store them in transparent negative sheets with the film number at the corner of the page. The sheets can then be inserted into a loose-leaf binder obtainable from most photographic shops, labelled for the appropriate subject. As each sheet is numbered to correspond with the number in the record book, it then becomes a simple matter to locate a particular negative. A full binder will hold around 80 sheets of negatives.

Transparencies

When I receive slides back from the processors I store them in slide boxes and keep a record in a master file (referring to my log book), numbering each transparency in date order (see Figure 7). Once I have done this I am free to take out the slides and put them into slide projector magazines for use in slide shows, but all the time I have a master record, so when I have finished with the slides it is an easy matter to transfer them back to the slide boxes.

Prints

Nowadays it is an easy matter to store prints. Albums of all sizes are now made in which prints can be slipped (face upwards) under a transparent sleeve, the back of the prints sticking to the page beneath. It is an easy matter to remove a print when required –the transparent cover is peeled back and the print eased from the gummed page.

Film No: BR 112, FP4, 125 ASA

Date	Place	Loco No	S/Sp	Ap	Conditions	Comments	Neg No
1/1/81	Bewdley SVR	43106	250	6.3	Bright	Light in stn	1
10/1/81	Ais Gill	D47106	500	4	Dullish	S'bound pass	2
2/2/81	All Stretton	6201	500	5.6	Sun	S'bound Welsh Marches	3
2/2/81	S of Hereford	4930	500	4	Bright	S'bound Welsh Marches	4

Figure 6: Record book layout

Date	Place	Loco No	Comments	Slide No
2/8/76	Lickey Bank	D45109	Sheffield train	1005
5/8/76	Carnforth	4472	On shed	1006
5/8/76	Carnforth	E86210	N'bound express	1007
6/8/76	Ravenglass	*River Irt*	Wtg to leave with Dalegarth tr	1008

Figure 7: Transparency master file

Alternatively fixed or loose-leaf pages with transparent pockets of various sizes can be used.

Care of equipment

Cameras and lenses

Every two weeks or so it is as well to check all the shutter speeds on your cameras, and also the delayed action lever. The slower shutter speeds may jam, especially if, as is so often the case, they are very rarely used. The same applies to lenses – check all the apertures from the widest to the smallest.

Make it a rule to clean all equipment after use, especially lens surfaces, and always carry a small brush to clean lenses while out on location. If your camera uses batteries, either for the meter or shutter or both, always carry spare batteries with you.

Projectors and enlargers

What applies to cameras and lenses applies equally to projectors and enlargers. For the best results always keep the equipment clean, especially the lenses and condensers. Special anti-static lens cloths can be bought at most photographic stores. Also always check the motion on the enlarger column, making sure that it works smoothly. Last but not least, always keep spare bulbs, which have a nasty habit of failing in the middle of a slide show or printing session.

Flash equipment

Always make sure that there is enough power for an evening's work by checking how long the unit takes to recharge after an exposure, and always carry spare batteries with you.

Submitting material for publication

Colour

For modern film-based or digital reproduction techniques, publishers prefer colour transparencies, although colour prints might be acceptable in certain circumstances – check

before submitting. Copy transparencies are sometimes not accepted. In the past publishers have tended to prefer the larger-size slide (6x6cm), but nowadays, with the high standard of 35mm cameras and lenses and high-quality colour emulsions, good-quality 35mm transparencies are quite acceptable provided they are clear, sharp and with good definition. Remember that whatever size you send to the publisher, always make sure that the picture has plenty of colour contrast and is correctly exposed.

Never send your slides mounted in glass (which can easily be broken in the post and so ruin the photograph) but use card or plastic mounts, and write your name and the subject matter clearly on each mount submitted. As most slides are fairly precious, it is as well to have copies made before sending them to publishers in case of loss.

Black and white

For monochrome work a black and white print is required. The print should be on glossy paper, preferably glazed, and the best print size is in the region of 16.5 x 21.6cm (8½ x 6½in) or 20.3 x 25.4cm (10 x 8in); any larger may cause the publisher storage difficulties.

Whatever size they are, make sure that, like transparencies, the prints are of good quality with plenty of contrast. Prints tend to lose a little in processing for printing, so it is important that they contain strong blacks and whites and good sharp detail.

Make sure that your name and the subject matter are on the back of every print, either on a label or written on the edge and away from any clear areas of the print, ie the sky; write clearly but lightly so as to avoid the print or label showing through on the emulsion side. With all material submitted, give as much detail of the subject matter as possible, for this will enable the editor to write a more detailed caption.

General points

Always make sure that all material is well packed before posting. It is advisable to mark the packet PHOTOGRAPHIC MATERIAL PLEASE DO NOT BEND. Slides can be sent in the processor's box. With regard to prints, insert a piece of card (a little larger than the prints)

A Birmingham to Wolverhampton EMU pulls out of Tipton on 1 July 1982 and passes a narrow boat on the Birmingham Canal. Note the contrast in modes of transport and how the picture is framed by the overbridge, and also how the reflections in the canal give depth to an otherwise elongated image. The verticals here are tricky since the bridge pier is not upright, the catenary masts are, and the train is on a canted curve.

Camera: Nikon FM with 50mm lens plus yellow filter. Exposure: 1/500th sec at f5.6. Film: Ilford XP1 rated at 400 ASA, developed in XP1 chemicals.

in the envelope with the photographs, which should suffice to keep the prints from being damaged. Publishers will expect you to enclose a stamped addressed envelope for the return of unwanted material, or they may not return it. Be patient and do not expect a reply immediately; most editors are very busy people and are probably having to look at hundreds of pictures and slides every week.

With regard to payment, most publishers have set rates of reproduction fees but some are by arrangement. Most publishers pay for reproduction use, and the copyright in the picture remains yours. If a publisher wants to buy outright copyright or claims it, be careful and make sure

you get adequate payment. Payment of reproduction fees is only usually made on publication of material and not on acceptance.

If your material is accepted, do not be discouraged if your pictures are not used immediately; features in magazines and books are planned well ahead and editors like to have a store of material from which to draw. Topical news pictures in contrast might find immediate use.

Learning more

Much can be learned about photography from joining a photographic club, where there are always experienced photographers on hand who are prepared to spend time in helping newcomers to overcome their photographic problems. Photographic clubs and societies contain many fine photographers and one can only improve by looking at their work and also by finding out the technical details of the photographs. Most fair-sized towns have a photographic club or society and details can usually be obtained from the local public library.

Another very useful move, especially for beginners, would be to enrol in a photographic course at a local night school. Here you would be shown the basics of developing a black and white film and printing the negatives. Some courses also deal with colour work. Night school courses are advertised in the local press and details can be obtained at the night schools concerned. These courses are usually run by experienced photographers and are generally good value for money.

In addition, read as many photographic books as you can. You can always benefit from learning about top photographers' style and technique. There are also weekly and monthly magazines like *Amateur Photographer* and *Practical Photography,* all of which abound in excellent tips and hints on all facets of photography, and of course there are many quality illustrated railway books and magazines.

Photographing abroad

Many railway photographers now travel overseas to see and photograph the railways of the world, particularly in the countries where steam locomotives are still used in any numbers. But whether you are travelling just across the water to France or as far afield as Africa, South America or the Far East, there are certain points worth bearing in mind.

Although film can be obtained in most countries, and in one or two places it may even be cheaper, it certainly pays to take enough with you, thus avoiding any problems that may arise. Processing can also be difficult abroad, so it is preferable to have your films processed when you get home.

Avoid allowing your film, whether exposed or unexposed, to pass through airport X-ray checks. No matter what people say, there is always a chance of the X-ray ruining your film and in consequence one of the main purposes of your holiday. Keep all your film separate from your cameras and ask for the film to be checked by hand. This may mean rewinding any unexposed film in your camera, but it could be well worth it in the long run. If you are using 120 size film you will lose a few frames, but with 35mm it is possible to use the rest of the film again. Make a note of the exposures taken, then rewind the film, but not completely into the cassette. There is a slight clicking sound as the film comes off the spool, and if you stop at that point the film leader will still be out of the cassette, thus enabling you to load the film again.

To reload the film in the camera, engage the film leader with the take-up spool, as normal, and close the back of the camera. Then, *most important of all*, place the lens cap on the lens, thus making the camera light-tight. Making a note of the frames already exposed, say 16, shoot off 19 exposures *with the cap still on the lens* – you will then be ready to expose the rest of the film in the normal way, having wasted only two or three exposures.

If possible always take a spare camera with you, for if your camera does break down the chances of getting it repaired are extremely remote, especially in some of the more exotic places that railway photographers get to.

Extremes of temperature can affect cameras and films. In very cold icy weather the camera shutter can be adversely

Class 27 No 27054 threads through Princes Street Gardens, Edinburgh, with the 10.30 train from Dundee on 5 June 1986. Side lighting has helped to create strong contrasting highlights, but great care was taken with the exposure to retain the detail in the shadow area. This was achieved by taking a light reading for both the shadow and the highlight areas, and using a balance of the two readings. Highlights were given extra exposure at the printing stage. Note the fine architecture of the building in the background, and how it balances the picture.

Camera: Nikon FM with 50mm lens.
Exposure: 1/500th sec at f5.6.
Film: Ilford XP1 rated at 400 ASA, developed in XP1 chemicals.

affected, and if you are photographing in such conditions keep your camera warm by carrying it inside a case or bag, only removing it just before taking a shot, then putting it away as soon as possible. Film can be affected by hot humid conditions as well as cold weather, so keep all film (when not in your camera) in plastic containers, which will certainly help to reduce any damage.

Finally, remember that not all countries accept that railway photographers are carrying out a harmless hobby. In a few extreme cases, even steam locomotives are among state property to be kept secret, and photographing them is tantamount to spying. Thus official permits might be required even if photographing at stations. On Britain's railways you should be able to take photographs anywhere where the public is normally permitted – with a ticket if necessary – but in these security-conscious days do not act irresponsibly, and be prepared to be challenged. Access to sheds, depots and other railway property will require a permit from the owner or operator.

Do's and don'ts

One of the most important things to remember with railway photography is that if you mess up a shot (and who has not?) it is extremely difficult to repeat it, and in some cases impossible. With this in mind, here is a final list of do's and don'ts.

- Make sure your camera is always loaded with film. This is not as silly as it sounds, and can happen to anyone, amateur or professional alike. After all, to take a photograph you have to be in the right location, with a camera – and with that camera loaded.

- If your camera has a built-in meter, be certain it is set to the correct film speed.

- Always wind on the film after taking the last exposure, which in most cameras re-cocks the shutter automatically. It is an awful feeling to have the 'master shot' in your viewfinder only to press the shutter release and find that nothing happens because the shutter release lock has not been reset. Also, make sure you have removed the lens cap.

- A point that comes up time and again in railway photography, simply because many pictures are taken from road bridges, is remembering to keep the camera clear of the parapet of the bridge. Many shots, particularly transparencies, have been marred because of this. No camera viewfinder gives you 100 per cent of the field of vision.

- Always use a lens hood. It may not always matter when taking a shot with the sun behind you, but it is important when you turn quickly to take a three-quarter rear shot and find yourself shooting against the sun. It also acts as some protection against rain and snow.

- If your camera uses batteries, always keep spare ones handy.

- Never get in the way of other photographers. This nearly always happens when people are chasing special trains. Everyone is in position for their shot when, just before the train arrives, up comes someone who runs into everyone's picture. People then shout at the interloper to move, which in turn can cause obvious problems for people doing sound recording, who by that time have very often started to film their sequence. Because of somebody's thoughtlessness many films are spoiled.

- Keep all unexposed films in a cool dry place, and process film as soon as possible after exposure.

- Finally, before taking your photograph adopt a firm stance, take a good deep breath and hold it until you have taken your shot. This will help to cut down on camera shake.

Glossary

Aperture The circular opening in a camera lens that controls the amount of light reaching the film. The size of the lens opening is indicated by the f number (qv). The higher the f number, the smaller the opening and therefore the less light; the lower the f number, the wider the opening and the greater the amount of light striking the film. Each higher full aperture f number allows half the light of its adjacent lower number – f11 is half of f8, f16 is half of f11, and so on.

ASA A term used to indicate film speed (qv). The lower the number, the slower the film, the higher the number, the faster the film. In practical terms, if a 50 ASA film is giving a shutter speed of 1/125th sec at f5.6, the equivalent exposure if using 100 ASA film will be 1/125th sec at f8, or 1/250th sec at f5.6. Therefore 100 ASA film is twice as fast as 50 ASA, 200 ASA is twice as fast as 100 ASA, and so on.

Average metering Taking meter readings from elements of the whole scene and evaluating to assess the exposure.

'B' The shutter speed setting at which the shutter will remain open as long as the release is held down.

Compact camera A small 35mm camera with a fixed lens.

Depth of field The distance between the nearest and furthest points of the subject that are acceptably sharp. Depth of field increases with the higher aperture f numbers, and decreases with the lower f numbers.

DIN The continental system for indicating the speed of films (see ASA above). 15 DIN = 25 ASA; 18 DIN = 50 ASA; 19 DIN = 64 ASA; 21 DIN = 100 ASA; 22 DIN = 125 ASA; 24 DIN = 200 ASA; 27 DIN = 400 ASA.

Exposure The total amount of light that reaches the film, controlled by the lens aperture and shutter speed.

Film speed The sensitivity of a film to light, usually measured in the terms of ASA or DIN numbers (qv). The lower the number, the slower the film, the higher the number, the faster the film.

Filter A glass or synthetic lens attachment used to alter the quality and amount of light passing through the lens.

f number A number indicating the aperture (opening) of the lens. Low numbers represent wide apertures and high numbers represent smaller apertures, usually in the progression f2.8, f4, f5.6, f8, f11, f16 and f22.

Focal length The distance between the rear nodal point of the lens and the focal plane (film plane) when the lens is focused on infinity.

Hot-shoe A camera fitting on which a flash gun may be mounted, enabling the flash unit to be fired simultaneously with the opening of the camera shutter.

Light meter A device for measuring light, to aid the determination of correct exposure.

Reciprocity failure A normal light meter gives accurate readings, with alternative equivalent settings for shutter and aperture in the daylight range of illumination. But in very dark conditions these equivalents fall out of step, and the meter cannot be relied upon for long exposures.

Self-timer A mechanical or electronic device that delays the firing of the shutter for up to 10 seconds after the photographer has pressed the shutter release – very useful for taking a self-portrait with your favourite locomotive!

Shutter The camera mechanism controlling the length of exposure.

Shutter speed The length of time that the shutter is open during exposure.

SLR Single lens reflex – a camera in which the photographer looks directly through the taking lens.

Standard lens A camera lens of a focal length (qv) approximating to the diagonal of the negative format. Also a lens that produces the most natural perspective image in relation to the picture area.

Telephoto lens A lens with a focal length greater than that of a standard lens.

TLR Twin lens reflex – a camera fitted with two lenses (of the same focal length) coupled together, one for taking the picture, the other for viewing and focusing.

TTL Through the lens – thus 'TTL metering' (metering through the lens), etc.

Wide angle lens A lens with a focal length less than that of a standard lens.

Zoom lens A lens with a variable focal length.

Index

Aperture 14, 127
Architecture, inclusion of 97
ASA ratings 127

'B' setting 113
Bridges and viaducts 74

Camera formats, 35mm 9,
    10
    6 x 4.5cm 9
    6 x 6cm 9
    6 x 7cm 9
Camera types, digital 11
    SLR 10
    TLR 10
    viewfinder 10
Camera shake 90
Cameras, care of 123
Cassettes, film 12
Colour photography 38
Composition, 33, 51
Contact sheets 24, 28

Darkroom 23
Depth of field 14, 127
Developers 24
Development 23
    films 23
    prints 24
Diesel traction 43
Digital photography 11
'Do's and don'ts' 126

Electric traction 45
Enlargers 33
    care of 123

Exposure meters 20
Exposures 12

Faults and remedies 116
Films 11
    black and white 11, 12
    colour negative (prints)
    12, 39
    colour reversal
    (transparencies) 11-12
Film/developer
    combinations 24
Film speed 11
Filters 18
    polarising 19
    red 19
    skylight 19
    ultraviolet 19
    yellow 19
Flash equipment, care of
    123
Flash photography 110
Footplate, photography
    from 90

Glazing 30
'Golden Section' 51
Gun pod 20

Landscapes 68
Lenses 12
    care of 123
    standard 12
    telephoto 14
    wide angle 14
    zoom 17

Lens converters 17
Lens hoods 20
Lighting 39, 105
    at night 113
    normal 107
    side and back 107
    silhouette 109

Miniature railways 45
Monopods 20
Motor drives 17

Negatives 23, 25
    developing 23
    storing 122
Night photography 110

Overseas photography 125

Panning and pacing 93
Photographic clubs and
    courses 124
Power winder 17
Printing paper 25-27
Prints (black and white),
    developing 24-30
    dodging 32
    double printing 33
    enlarging 24
    glazing 30
    mounting and
    presentation 36
    quality 34
    shading 32
    storing 122
    spotting 30

Projectors, care of 123
Publishing, submitting
    material for 123

Reading material 124
Records, keeping 122
Remedying faults 116

Sheds and depots 86
Shutter speeds 43, 93
Signals 80
Stations 82
Steam traction 41
Styles, photographic 50

Technique, photographic
    50
Test prints 25, 28
Time exposures 113
Towns and cities 72
Trains, photography from
    90
Tunnels and cuttings 77
Transparencies, storing
    122
Tripods 20, 113

Weather 99
    fog and mist 99
    rain 99
    snow 102
    wind 99

X-ray equipment 125